THE NEW BUREAUCRACY

Quality assurance and its critics

Max Travers

10272960

First published in Great Britain in 2007 by

The Policy Press
University of Bristol
Fourth Floor
Beacon House
Queen's Road
Bristol BS8 1QU
UK

Tel +44 (0)117 331 4054
Fax +44 (0)117 331 4093
e-mail tpp-info@bristol.ac.uk
www.policypress.org.uk

British Library Cataloguing in Publication Data
A catalogue record for this book is available from the British Library.

Library of Congress Cataloging-in-Publication Data
A catalog record for this book has been requested.

ISBN 978 1 86134 927 9 paperback
ISBN 978 1 86134 928 6 hardcover

Cover design by Qube Design Associates, Bristol.
Front cover photograph kindly supplied by Getty Images.
Printed and bound in Great Britain by Cromwell Press, Trowbridge.

To Dede Boden

Contents

Acknowledgements

This book reports the findings of a project that was completed over a relatively long period, and took shape after 2003 when I moved from the United Kingdom to Australia. I would like to thank the senior managers who gave me permission to interview inspectors and quality managers about their work, and practitioners for sharing their experiences of 'red tape'. I started to see the relevance of feedback forms to wider debates about modernity through teaching the Sociological Analysis of Modern Society (SAMS) at the University of Tasmania. I would like to thank my colleagues and students for their support, and for helping someone from a metropolitan background adjust to a completely different environment.

Although they are not responsible for the content, I am grateful to Peter Wilkins and Richard Harding for their advice during a visit to Perth; to Kevin Stenson, Emily Hansen, Rod Watson, Paul Watt and Harry Travers for their suggestions; and to Keith Jacobs, Ellie and Iolanthe Francis-Brophy, Reza Banakar, Lyn Burden, Janet Entwistle, Denise Farran, Jon Mulberg and Anjana Bhattarcharjee for their friendship and support. I am also grateful to The Policy Press for its editorial work and designing the cover. I have dedicated this book to Dede Boden (1940-2001), a sociologist and friend who encouraged me to pursue this project.

Max Travers
November 2006

ONE

Introduction

In some senses, this book is an attempt to understand the humble feedback form. You may have encountered one while taking courses at university or, perhaps, after being discharged from hospital or receiving help from the police. In universities, students are asked to spend a few minutes ticking boxes or assigning a numerical grade to such statements as 'The course met the objectives set' and offering comments or suggestions. The figures are converted into tables of percentage scores by a central department and used in the university to assess performance. They may even be posted on a website, and be referred to in aggregate terms in government reports comparing the performance of different universities.

Although many people complete these forms without giving them a second thought, it is interesting to consider that they are a relatively recent development. University courses were delivered and assessed during the 1970s without using them, and there was far less emphasis on measuring or improving quality in public sector agencies. More generally, quality assurance has only recently emerged as an occupation, or sub-field, of management. Today, there are many complaints by public sector professionals about the damaging effects of bureaucracy and 'red tape' created by this new form of regulation. On the one hand, government remains committed to improving the delivery of public services. To use a phrase often found in press releases issued by the civil service, the aim is to 'drive up' standards in health, education and criminal justice. On the other hand, professionals and other public sector workers often complain about a burden of paperwork caused by form filling, report writing and preparation for inspections (Power, 1997; O'Neill, 2002; Marquand, 2004). There is also resentment against what is perceived to be an ever-expanding bureaucracy created by quality assurance, including staff employed to prepare for inspections and maintain quality procedures.

This book will consider the conceptual and political issues raised by attempts to measure quality from a sociological perspective that is interested in day-to-day work and everyday experience. Although there have been some thought-provoking academic books about these issues, the authors write in general terms about society, employing abstract concepts such as risk, trust or governmentality, rather than looking at the concerns and problems of the people promoting or implementing quality assurance initiatives, or their effect on particular organisations. They also tell us little about what people actually do at work, whether these are inspectors charged with measuring the quality of performance in some organisation, or the professionals who deliver public services.

The aim of this book is to get inside quality assurance, both in the sense of an occupation and new form of regulation. Ideally, for such a project, one would want access to a wide range of people and institutions, and the opportunity to interview practitioners, managers and civil servants at length about their day-to-day work and occupational perspectives. One would also want to observe what actually happens when inspectors deliberate about the performance of an institution, or professionals review issues about quality, or managers discuss concerns about the performance of professionals. It is by spending time in what the American sociologist Erving Goffman (1959) called these 'backstage' settings that one can gain most insight into what people understand by the term 'quality'.

Inevitably, this study falls short of obtaining this level of access to public sector organisations. Like many professionals, the author has experienced an inspection visit and attended meetings concerned with planning or discussing how to frame a response to a quality report. It was not, however, possible to obtain permission to observe an inspection, or interview inspectors or those being inspected during this process at any level of detail. The impression gained in approaching both inspectorates and agencies subject to inspection was not that they are unsympathetic to research, or worried that an independent observational study might present them in a bad light.[1] The problem is more that public agencies, placed under a great deal of pressure to achieve targets, do not wish to take on the additional burden of facilitating a research project. One inspectorate complained of having only a small office to conduct a large programme of inspections while having to face the demands of two civil service reviews.[2] The management team of a division within one public organisation that was preparing for an inspection believed that the presence of a researcher would lead to 'greater pressure', and might affect its grade.

It is easier to obtain permission to interview people generally about their work, and later chapters draw on interviews with quality assurance officers, inspectors and managers, and with professionals who welcomed the opportunity to report their experiences of what one described as 'pointless bureaucracy', and being tied up by 'red tape'. Some of the best studies in the symbolic interactionist tradition have been based on the analysis of 30 interviews with some occupational group. However, it is also possible to learn a great deal from even a single interview, and one problem with policy research, and sociological research more generally at present, is that we do not usually listen with much care to what interviewees say, or reveal, about their own lives.

In addition to interviews, there are many public sources of information about quality assurance. There are, for example, numerous official reports about quality scandals in the United Kingdom, and reports about these in the media. There are literally thousands of reports by inspectorates published each year about different organisations. Although one could complain that these only provide an official, managerial view of how public sector organisations work, they are nonetheless valuable sources of data on different occupational perspectives, and the practical issues that concern managers. Then there are the different views about quality assurance found in management guides and professional journals.

Finally, this book is also informed by the author's own experience of working in higher education, and seeing how quality assurance developed in Britain during the 1990s. Reflecting on one's own life for sociological purposes is hard to do, particularly when one tries to describe what is involved in routine professional work or administrative procedures. This book aims to supply some detail that is not usually reported in the social policy literature on what quality means as a practical issue to those working in higher education, without claiming that this is a definitive view.

Drawing on these various materials, the book aims to convey a straightforward, descriptive account of quality assurance in the British public sector that documents with different degrees of insight and detail the work involved in maintaining this form of regulation, and how it affects professionals. The sociological tradition that has most influenced this approach to investigating work is symbolic interactionism, and particularly the naturalistic approach to studying work developed by Everett Hughes (1971) and his students during the 1940s and 1950s at the University of Chicago. Hughes was interested in the nature of different perspectives, such as those of managers, professionals and clients, who will necessarily understand the issue of quality differently. This study has also been influenced by ethnomethodology, the tradition developed by Harold Garfinkel (1984, 2002) at the University of California in Los Angeles during the same period. This provides a set of analytic and methodological resources that allows one to describe just what is involved in conducting a scientific experiment, interacting with a computer or playing jazz piano. It does not tell the researcher how to proceed in any study, other than to say that one must respect the lived 'in vivo' character of the activity, which in this case includes how professionals understand the issue of quality and competence, and how people accomplish routine administrative tasks.

Chapter Two starts by looking at the origins of quality assurance, and how it has developed and continues to prosper and expand as a new occupation. Although it is easy to assume that something like quality assurance has been around forever, in fact it is a relatively recent development. Our ideas about quality, and the whole apparatus used to measure performance in the public sector can be traced back to a small group of American management thinkers writing in the 1970s and 1980s, and particularly W. Edwards Deming. Their ideas not only became a powerful movement in manufacturing industry, but were also taken up by governments and have rapidly spread around the world. The current emphasis on quality and accountability also results from the success of a reforming movement inside government during the 1980s that has resulted in what has become known as the new public management. The chapter also argues that the expansion of quality assurance as a social movement is made possible through constructing professional work as a problem. A good example is the inquiry into the deaths of children at the Bristol Royal Infirmary that resulted in the creation of a new health inspectorate.

Chapter Three looks at how professionals understand the issue of quality, and why they are generally hostile towards quality assurance. It begins by reviewing the arguments that have been made for and against the professions, and the recent analysis by Elliot Freidson (2001) on the decline of professions against the forces of the market and state. The chapter also considers the neglected topic of professionalism: how professionals understand the issue of quality, and make this visible in their day-to-day work. Drawing on empirical research in a law firm, and the author's own experience in higher education, it considers how quality is understood and demonstrated in these work settings. Professionals often have a feeling of moral superiority, both in relation to their clients, and also to other professional groups. Their work also often involves judgement and discretion, so any two practitioners may have different, strongly held, views on quality. This explains why professionals dislike quality assurance since this questions the motives and practices of professionals, and claims that performance can be measured using objective criteria.

Chapter Four looks at quality assurance from the perspective of government. It examines the methods developed to make public sector organisations accountable, which include requiring them to measure their progress using performance indicators, and the comparison of performance across institutions through league tables. The second half of the chapter also looks at the work of inspectorates, the methodologies they employ, and the practical work of making quality judgements, drawing on interviews with inspectors. It concludes by considering the growth of evaluation as a requirement made on public sector agencies, and how all these activities are informed by the goal of continuous improvement.

Chapter Five looks at the impact of auditing and inspection on public sector organisations, focusing on the work and perspective of managers. They are required, but also have a genuine desire, to improve performance and do this by writing mission statements, setting targets and trying to measure whether these have been attained through performance indicators. In some cases, organisations apply for accreditation from quality schemes such as ISO 9000 or a Chartermark award from the British government. They also have to prepare for inspections by external agencies that can be consequential. The rest of this chapter looks at the effects of these initiatives in three organisations: two universities that illustrate variations in quality assurance procedures within a particular occupation; and a police force. It considers the claim made by managers in public sector agencies that they suffer from over-regulation.

Chapter Six considers how professionals experience and understand 'red tape' through interviewing general practitioners, nurses, lawyers and university lecturers, and considering what is involved in completing quality assurance forms. The interviews show that not everyone regards this as burdensome, but that quality assurance has created new administrative tasks for professionals, and takes up a great deal of time. The impersonal and bureaucratic features of forms and procedures themselves can produce frustration and anxiety. It is suggested that people who complain about bureaucracy and 'red tape' often relate this to wider concerns about the impact of structural changes in how services are delivered on professionalism.

Chapter Seven adopts a broader perspective by considering how academic writers present quality assurance as a problem, and how this relates to wider debates about industrialisation and modernity. It reviews the criticisms made by Michael Power (1997) and Onora O'Neill (2002), and relates these to the arguments advanced by the tradition of labour process studies in Marxism and the Foucauldian neo-governmentality tradition. One difficulty for critics is where to stand in relation to professional expertise. Many sociologists have criticised professional power in the past, but complain when they are subject to regulation.

This is the author's second attempt to address a contentious public issue from an interpretive perspective. *The British immigration courts* (Travers, 1999) looked at the work of appeals tribunals in recognising refugees, and described how it is often very difficult reaching a decision (which one might also expect to find in attempts to measure quality). Institutional arrangements in Britain concerning immigration control have been criticised because it can take years to reach a decision, and there are no resources to remove unsuccessful appellants. In addition, many believe that the emphasis placed on measuring and assuring quality is pathological because the administrative burdens may actually damage the institutions delivering services, by creating additional tiers of management, and unnecessary paperwork for overworked professionals.

British governments are not alone in trying to measure the quality of public services, and this book raises wider issues about scientific management, and the tension between the professions and state that have interested many sociological theorists. In some respects, quality assurance can be seen as a social movement that started in Britain and America, and has since become a globalising force (Pollitt and Bouckaert, 2004), although one can only speculate on the mechanisms of transmission. There is, for example, nothing like the same concern in Australia with quality assurance or performance management in public sector organisations, and almost no inspectorates. Nevertheless, organisations like universities and hospitals are increasingly introducing quality assurance measures, often modelled on those in Britain, or drawing on American management theory, so this book should interest anyone affected by these developments.

There are, of course, many critical sociologists who will want to read the materials presented in this book politically. A number of writers in both the Marxist and Foucauldian traditions have sought to explain the rise of quality assurance in the restructuring of public services associated with neo-liberalism. Other critics such as Michael Power emphasise the ritualistic character of quality assurance, and how it potentially damages public sector agencies. This book supplies evidence and examples that can be used to make a similar case against quality assurance. However, it should be made clear from the outset that there are no easy remedies, just as there are no simple or cost-free solutions to achieving a fairer or more effective system of immigration control. The rationalistic belief that everything can be measured and improved has deep roots in our intellectual culture, so it is difficult thinking of what might replace quality assurance, or prevent it from spreading internationally in societies where an increasing proportion of the workforce is employed in administrative or managerial jobs.

Instead of advancing a political argument against quality assurance, the book focuses on three questions that have not been addressed by other academic writers. The first is what we actually do at work, and how we experience bureaucracy as an unpleasant but necessary and unavoidable part of our working lives. This receives less attention than it should in theoretical discussions of modernity. To give one example, Richard Sennett (2006) in an otherwise compelling book argues that 'pyramidal bureaucracy' no longer exists, whereas anyone working in the public sector knows that it is in robust and vigorous health. The second is the gap between measurement and reality: the extent to which the objective measures favoured by governments can assess the quality of public sector work or address what really matters. The third is the difference in perspective between managers and professionals, which is complicated by the fact that management is a profession and professionals are often managers. Harold Garfinkel (2002) has argued that the 'formal analytic' procedures in social science cannot address the world as it happens, or the gritty, practical details that matter to people in actual social settings but disappear once we start to theorise about them. This book is written partly as an interpretive contribution to the sociology of work and occupations, but also in the hope of generating discussion and greater awareness, particularly among public sector managers and professionals themselves, of the problems created by this new form of regulation.

Notes

[1] When the author interviewed a district auditor, she had to obtain permission from her superiors in the office upstairs for the interview to be tape-recorded, and this was granted only on condition that they received a copy of the tape.

[2] See Office of Public Services Reform (2003). The 2005 Budget announced that the 11 public service inspectorates would be reduced to four by 2008. According to the Cabinet Office (2005), 'the strategy is to re-focus, rationalise and reduce the volume of inspection' and reduce the burden on professionals.

Quality assurance as a new occupation

This chapter starts with some general observations about the problems involved in understanding the origins of something as all pervasive but diffuse as quality assurance. It then considers how this new occupation or industry has developed in Britain and America, looking at both manufacturing industry and the public sector. It will become apparent that Britain has been substantially influenced by ideas developed in America, and in particular by the quality movement promoted by W. Edwards Deming and his associates in the early 1980s. However, the influence is by no means one-way, and the chapter aims to show that Britain still has a distinctive approach to assuring quality in the public sector based on central regulation and control. The second half of the chapter will examine how quality assurance has expanded through constructing professional work as a social problem. It concludes by offering an overview of those institutions and processes that seem sociologically interesting and are considered in more detail in later chapters.

The origins of quality assurance

One disconcerting, and yet comforting, feature of human societies is that governing ideas and values change relatively quickly, so that what to one generation seems self-evident and unquestionable can be challenged and then completely forgotten within a period of years. For the victors, it is tempting to write up history as a narrative of inevitable triumph of enlightenment over ignorance. Michel Foucault's archaeological approach to intellectual history (1967, 1977) brilliantly shows how this is never true of what actually happens. Similarly, Thomas Kuhn (1962) showed how scientific revolutions only really succeed when the old order retires and can no longer block the dissemination of new ideas. In fact, all careful history shows that the triumph of some cause can take many years, often depends on unexpected or contingent events, and did not seem at all inevitable at the time.

The triumph of quality assurance can be demonstrated by the fact that it is all around us, to the extent that we take its existence largely for granted. On the inside sole of a pair of shoes it is common to find a circular sticker stating 'quality assured', presumably to reassure the customer, if not already persuaded by this company's advertising and brand image, that they are buying a good product. Similar stickers can be found on apples, giving a numerical code that suggests someone has checked each item of fruit. In some restaurants, it is common to be asked if you have enjoyed the meal, sometimes more than once. Similarly, there is always a feedback form on the bedside table in hotel rooms, and some hotels send this by email after the trip with a polite message asking you to spare a 'few minutes' for the sake of future customers. Inside restrooms in businesses and public buildings, there will often be a sign stating that the facilities are checked every hour for quality assurance purposes, indicating when and by whom they were last checked.

These are unremarkable, everyday examples of a concern with quality one would not have found 20 years ago, and they are only the surface indications of major changes that have taken place in the way companies manufacture goods or deliver services, and of the importance of measuring and assessing performance in all kinds of settings. As Michel Foucault has noted in relation to changes that took place in social institutions like hospitals and prisons, albeit over a much longer period, there is no obvious centre to these developments, and many different practices, and in his terminology 'technologies', may be involved. The same point has been made elegantly by other French poststructuralists, including Bruno Latour (1995) and Gilles Deleuze (1995), reacting against the relatively simple, or in the case of Marxist thought, economically deterministic, understanding of historical change by a previous generation of historians and social theorists.

Ultimately, quality assurance must, along with the rest of our civilisation, have something to do with the optimistic belief expressed with great eloquence and force by 18th-century European thinkers like Voltaire and Condorcet that the application of reason and science will result in a better world. It must also have something to do with the immense economic and social changes, described by the classical sociologists, that still affect us today: the transition from a society where most people worked on the land, and human life was often brutish and short, to our affluent, industrialised, consumer society (Polyani, 1957; Berman, 1983). Improving the quality of life systematically, through the application of science in different fields, has become a central objective for government and commercial organisations. Quality assurance can be understood in these terms as simply arising from, or constituting, along with other intellectual, cultural and institutional movements, the modern world. However, this still leaves the question as to how it has developed as a specialist occupation so rapidly in recent years, and whether it has been successful in achieving a good quality of life.

Although it would theoretically be possible to write an archaeological history of how quality assurance has developed over the past few decades, in practice it would be difficult. This is partly because one is dealing with two areas of social life, industry and government, which, while supposedly public, in practice take place behind closed doors in places like the Cabinet Office or the boardrooms of large companies or seminars run by management consultants. It also quickly becomes apparent in interviewing managers or civil servants that all institutions have short memories. Even one year down the line, it is not unusual for the circumstances in which some important decision was made to have become irrelevant to current issues and problems. This is particularly apparent in studying the British civil service, where officials are regularly moved around, and new teams formed to continue some initiative. Even when people remain in post, the past is quickly forgotten or idealised. This is why books about the history of quality assurance or the new public sector management, some of which have been written by relative insiders, are frustrating or unsatisfying if you are interested in how decisions were actually made.

There is, however, an additional problem in studying the rise of something like quality assurance, in that most of the key people involved in promoting and introducing new ideas are anonymous or difficult to find. The history of public administration is harder to write than natural science where one can speak to the scientists working in a particular field and follow the reception of their work (for example, Collins and Pinch, 1982; Lynch, 1985; Latour and Woolgar, 1986). In the case of quality assurance, we know little about the consultants who developed the quality industry in the United Kingdom, or their dealings with government departments. We also know little about the civil servants and senior managers who have transformed public administration over 30 years. This chapter does not, therefore, provide a history of quality assurance based on primary source materials. Instead, it offers an interpretation based on the few historical and sociological accounts available of how quality assurance developed in the two countries (see also Pollitt, 1990; Wilkinson and Willmott, 1995; Strathern, 2000).

The American experience: an evangelical movement

Quality first developed as a concern for American manufacturing in the late 1970s as companies realised they were falling behind the Japanese in producing reliable, high-quality goods. This has resulted in a set of models or systems that are promoted internationally by consultants, the most successful of which is total quality management or TQM (another being 'business process re-engineering'). During the 1980s, the Reagan government set out to improve the effectiveness of government agencies, and over time the movement successfully promoted itself to public sector institutions through books like Osborne and Gaebler's (1993) *Reinventing government*.

The quality movement in manufacturing

The Japanese economic miracle that took place during the 1950s was largely due to the strategic opportunities that were available in rebuilding a set of industries from scratch after the Second World War. What impressed overseas visitors, however, was the different culture of production that was evident the moment one visited a Japanese factory. According to some texts promoting the new approach during the 1970s, workers and managers barely spoke to each other in America, and despite periodic efforts to improve productivity, there was stubborn resistance in most workforces (Tsutsui, 1998). The time and motion approach to setting goals and rewarding performance devised by Frederick Taylor in the 1920s, and the subsequent attempt by the human relations school to create cultures of productivity, had both failed (Pollitt, 1993, ch 1). In Japan, by contrast, everyone worked together harmoniously and with apparent real enthusiasm for work, focusing on how procedures could be continually improved to satisfy the customer.

Some American management consultants had been invited over to Japan in the early 1950s to advise on how to develop this new system of production. Although originally not well known in America, they attracted a large following during the 1980s when it became clear that America was performing poorly in exporting manufactured goods, and they offered a way to restore competitiveness through improving quality using Japanese methods (Tsutsui, 1998). The best-known figure, whose writings are regularly cited in books about improving quality in the British public sector, is W. Edwards Deming, although other pioneers include Joseph Juran, Walter Shewhart and Armand Feigenbaum. Deming was enthusiastically discovered as a potential saviour of American industry after giving a television interview in 1980, and became the first of many self-styled management gurus to have attracted large followings, particularly in the United States, but also internationally.[1]

Deming, like earlier innovators in American industry, had originally trained as an engineer and was a statistician. Although this aspect of his work is often forgotten, he placed great emphasis on the scientific measurement of the quality of production processes using sampling techniques. However, he is best known for suggesting that inspection after the event cannot substantially improve quality. Instead, industries needed to develop cultures among managers and shopfloor workers to prevent problems from arising. Considering how quality assurance has developed in the public sector, it is interesting that advocates of TQM argued that organisations with a separate quality assurance department are not sufficiently serious about quality improvement:

> Another basic TQM precept is that the responsibility for quality is not restricted to an organization's quality assurance department, but is instead a guiding philosophy shared by everyone in an organisation.... By relying on inspection (or detection, rather than prevention), most of these organisations have unknowingly and unwittingly instilled a deep belief in the people who actually manufacture products that they are no longer responsible for the quality of their output. TQM means this thinking is reversed, and everyone takes responsibility for quality.

> Does this type of thinking work? Absolutely. Most of us would intuitively suspect that in order to improve quality, the quality assurance department would have to grow. In companies that successfully implement TQM just the opposite occurs.... If everyone is responsible for the quality of the output (and everyone accepts this responsibility), the need for a separate quality assurance function disappears. (Berk and Berk, 1993, p 7)

Deming also recommended that companies abolish appraisals, which have since become a central task of management, and concentrate on improving systems and training (Deming, 1986; Voehl, 1995).[2] The argument here was that setting individual goals would produce negative effects unless measures were taken to address the systemic problems that result in poor quality. Although it is not explicitly stated, there is also an implied disapproval of management as a paper-producing bureaucracy that holds back companies when managers and workers should together be focusing on quality.

Another central idea was 'benchmarking', which involved continually monitoring what competitors were doing, and 'incorporating their wisdom into your organisation' (Berk and Berk, 1993, p 11). Remodelling a company in this way also meant giving workers more say in decision making, perhaps through setting up quality councils that replaced hierarchical management structures. Deming also recommended that companies should reduce the natural 'variability' in product quality through listening to customers:

> Feedback from customers of their experience of product and service quality, as well as from monitoring of internal processes, is essential in evaluating variability and ensuring customer satisfaction. (Ebel, 1991, p 18)

Perhaps the most radical idea promoted to American manufacturing with energy and self-belief by Deming and his associates was that for quality to be sustained in a continually changing marketplace there had to be 'continuous improvement':

> Improvement is an ongoing effort which focuses on all aspects of the organisation including financial and human resource management; administration, production and management processes; products and services; relationships

with customers and suppliers; and relationships between departments and between people. (Ebel, 1991, p 7)

The reinvention of government

There have been complaints about the poor levels of service provided by American government agencies since the 1960s. By the late 1970s, most states were experiencing fiscal problems: they could not afford to deliver basic services. However, attempts to raise taxation led to protest movements by middle-class taxpayers. California voters secured a freeze on taxes through Proposition 13 in 1978. This forced administrators to consider ways of improving services without spending more money. For similar reasons, the national administrations of Ronald Reagan during the 1980s, and Bill Clinton during the 1990s, became interested in improving performance.

The most influential text of this movement is David Osborne and Ted Gaebler's (1993) *Reinventing government*. Gaebler was a city administrator who became a consultant, and Osborne was a Washington journalist described in the book as 'a tireless evangelist for efficiency in government'. The book was partly an argument for the privatisation of government services, or at least the introduction of market competition, and the reduction of central regulation and 'red tape'. The authors also promoted the idea that every organisation needs a mission statement, should obtain feedback from customers and constantly measure performance.

Competition was presented as something that would always result in a higher level of service. The authors gave the example of an in-house stationery store in Minnesota that was forced to cut bureaucracy, speed up delivery and stock a wider range of goods when it lost its position as monopoly supplier. Refuse collection was delivered cheaper and faster in Phoenix through using trucks with a larger capacity and planning more efficient routes. In this case, workers were not laid off, since there was an agreement to move them to private contractors if they obtained the contract. However, the delivery of the service was improved through a new commitment to 'continuous improvement' that was required to survive in a competitive market.

A second suggestion made by Osborne and Gaebler was that the bureaucratic rules and 'red tape' that prevented agencies from innovating should be removed. Many of these originated during the Prohibition era as attempts to fight corruption but now prevented managers from making local decisions:

> The price we pay is staggering. Rule-driven government may prevent some corruption, but at the price of massive waste. Who can put a price tag on the employees who have given up? Who can put a price tag on the bureaucracies that grow ever larger, because they are so locked up by rules and line items that they cannot do anything new without adding more people and more resources? (Osborne and Gaebler, 1993, p 112)

Instead of this unnecessary regulation, agencies should pursue missions focused on serving the needs of customers. The idea of having a mission statement did not originate with this book, but with the quality movement in manufacturing in which managers were advised to have clear objectives and communicate these to employees. However, it illustrates how the ideas spread during the 1980s from private industry to the public sector, and are now taken for granted by schools, hospitals and higher education institutions across the world. Osborne and Gaebler argued that devising a mission statement that focused on quality and customer service could increase morale among public sector workers and lead to a dramatic improvement in service delivery.

Although they were committed to reducing bureaucracy, Osborne and Gaebler also argued that some new administrative measures were required to produce quality. One of these was obtaining feedback from customers. They would ideally have liked to give customers the ability to choose between service providers, the only real guarantee that feedback would be taken seriously (Osborne and Gaebler, 1993, p 180). However, a good step in this direction was what they called 'listening to the voice of the customer'. They gave the example of a police department in Madison that started mailing questionnaires to every 50th person it had dealings with, including offenders:

> Every month, more than two hundred people receive the survey, which comes with a postage-paid, self-addressed return envelope. It asks them to rate the officers they encountered on seven factors: concern; helpfulness; knowledge; quality of service; professional conduct; how well they solved the problem; and whether they put the person at ease. They can rate an officer 'excellent', 'good', 'fair', 'poor' or 'very poor'. An open-ended question asks: 'How can we improve the quality of our service in the future?'.

Forty percent of the recipients return the survey – a figure the department reached only after Chief David Couper started including a hand-written note explaining that he personally reads every survey. Couper publishes the results in the departmental newsletter and sends positive comments along to the officers who receive them. On a scale in which 3 is 'fair' and 4 is 'good', the department has increased its average rating from 3.8 to 4.3. (Osborne and Gaebler, 1993, p 173)

More generally, Osborne and Gaebler stressed the importance of measurement and evaluation, so that performance was improved using scientific methods. If this information were fed back to the workforce, it would enable them to improve quality. It is interesting, given what has happened since, that these pioneers of quality assurance opposed the introduction of performance-related pay on the grounds that it involved subjective judgements by managers that 'can easily degenerate into subjectivity and favoritism' (Osborne and Gaebler, 1993, p 157), lead to employees pursuing volume targets (for example, the number of arrests per officer in a police force), or simply create stress and anxiety. However, they believed that work groups and successful organisations should be rewarded. There should, for example, be a way of comparing schools that took account of different socioeconomic intakes, but still encouraged them to improve their performance.

An assessment

The success of TQM in America, which like other commercial products has diversified into a number of brands, was partly due to the anxieties of companies at a time when business seemed to be failing, and the evangelical zeal with which it was promoted by charismatic figures like Deming. It also quickly became institutionalised in management schools, and promoted through a number of associations that ran conferences and training events, such as the American Society for Quality. Finally, although the details remain unclear, the quality movement advanced by recruiting key allies in powerful companies and government agencies. The American government promoted and legitimated this new conception of management through setting up an annual prize, the Malcolm Baldrige National Quality Award (see Milakovich, 1995, p 175).

Inevitably there have been cynics and detractors who have questioned whether reorganising companies on these lines actually achieves anything (Garvin, 1991; Wilkinson and Willmott, 1995). Despite tens of thousands of managers having taken seminars run by quality gurus, and numerous initiatives, the American economy is still deeply uncompetitive and the trade deficit is wider than ever (Tenner and DeToro, 1992, ch 1; Associated Press, 2005). The Japanese economy, despite its superior management methods, collapsed during the 1990s and is only just starting to recover, and other countries have overtaken it in producing high-quality manufactured goods without using the same methods. One can also see how a school or police force might object to the emphasis on using customer feedback to document performance, and that collecting this information runs the risk of creating bureaucratic procedures that are every bit as stifling or demotivating as central regulation. It is significant that this second potential problem was not even considered by Osborne and Gaebler. They had complete faith that quality could be measured without significant cost.

Finally, it is worth noting that the quality movement has some features in common with other successful movements concerned with individual self-improvement in American social life (for example, Rogers, 1983; Robbins, 1997). Quality products are promoted by charismatic speakers at seminars that employ some of the techniques used by Alcoholics Anonymous or in religious revivalist meetings. There may not be anything equivalent to the 10-step programmes used to generate and maintain motivation, and, in the case of some self-improvement groups, raise income, or the promise of joining an inner circle found in some cult-like organisations. Nevertheless, the packaging of information into a set of simple principles (Deming's 14 points or Crosby's 14 steps) is similar to the way in which other self-improvement movements sell their wares. There is also no way of proving that TQM does not work.[3] As the manuals suggest, failure to achieve results can be explained by the failure of a 'critical mass' of employees to adopt the principle of making quality central to their work. The TQM literature also recognises that those trying to establish a new way of working will face opposition from vested interests, and that any company that adopts its principles will not change overnight.

The British experience: bureaucratic regulation

Despite these criticisms, one cannot deny that this American social movement has been successful in changing the way managers in all kinds of organisations understand their work. Terms like 'benchmarking', 'continuous improvement' and 'customer feedback' are often used in the British public sector, even though one gets little sense of the radical, evangelical spirit of the American pioneers. There have been fewer programmes designed to democratise decision making and release energy and creativity through establishing quality circles; and rather more emphasis on establishing new rule books and bureaucratic procedures. Instead of evangelical zeal, one gets what is perhaps best described as bureaucratic regulation.

For most of the 20th century, government had direct control over key industries, and closely supervised the delivery of public services through inspectorates based in the departments of state. During the 1970s, the task of setting and ensuring compliance with standards was effectively privatised into an industry coordinated through the British Standards Institute (Kirkpatrick and Martinez Lucio, 1995, pp 5-6). The most important development was the reform programme within government known as the new public management in the 1980s, which compelled a wide range of bodies, from local authorities to police forces, to place more emphasis on accountability and quality.[4] This has resulted in a dense system of multiple regulation where public sector organisations have set up internal procedures to measure and assure quality, but are also inspected by a number of government bodies, as well as seeking accreditation through different private schemes.

The inspectorates

The British government's system of inspectorates started in the 19th century with the Factory Acts, which sought to improve health and safety at work. This was, however, only the first of what became a characteristically British form of governmental regulation. Schools inspection dates back to 1839 and Her Majesty's Inspectorate of Police was established in 1856. There are currently 11 public service inspectorates that include the Adult Learning Inspectorate, the Benefit Fraud Inspectorate, Her Majesty's Crown Prosecution Inspectorate, the Office for Standards in Education (Ofsted) and the Audit Commission Inspection Service.

During the 19th and most of the 20th century, inspectorates mainly provided expert advice, and a means of sharing best practice across the country (Day and Klein, 1990). Today, they are expected to produce information that allows citizens to evaluate the services they are receiving, or, in the case of schools and hospitals, shop around, so that a poorly performing institution may face closure. The reports prepared by inspectorates are public documents available from their websites. In addition, government departments have developed sophisticated methods of collecting performance information, and publish their own league tables (Carter et al, 1992). This has been taken furthest in primary and secondary school education, where it is possible for parents to compare success rates in national tests and examinations. Similar information is now available to the public on government websites about hospitals, local authorities, police forces and universities.

The British Standards Institute and accreditation

John Seddon (2000, ch 1) provides an informative account of how quality assurance developed in Britain. An important difference with America is that many key industries were nationalised during the post-war Attlee government. This meant that the coal industry, electricity and atomic energy were all directly managed by government departments. Initiatives to improve quality in Britain came from the government, rather than the private sector, and have often been imposed on managers working in nationalised industries who have opposed the need for additional regulation.

Whereas the last thing quality assurers in American industry wanted was to create a central bureaucratic agency that would monitor and enforce standards, this is precisely what happened in Britain, although the mechanism became accreditation rather than inspection. During the 1950s and 1960s, there were a series of scandals about problems in the manufacture of turbine blades, boilers and components in the nuclear industry, which was then publicly owned. This resulted in the government promoting a 'Quality and Reliability Year' in 1966, and imposing requirements for these industries to check the components received from private suppliers.

Initially, inspectors based in central departments were given the task of ensuring that companies had proper systems in place. The Raby committee in 1969, however, suggested that independent consulting organisations were better equipped to develop common standards, and the inspectorates were effectively privatised. This new industry created its own association, the British Standards Institute (BSI), in which techniques to measure and assess quality were discussed and developed, and parties were brought together to negotiate common standards across particular industries. In 1971, the BSI published the first national standard for quality in the electronics industry, BS 9000. It was not, however, until 1979, after extensive consultations with government and industry, that a national quality standard was agreed, BS 5750. In 1987, the British Standard was adopted as the standard promoted to the world business community by the International Organisation for Standardisation, ISO 9000.

To obtain ISO 9000 certification, a company has to set up a system that measures quality, identifies and remedies problems, and above all documents that this is taking place. Seddon provides a summary of the key elements:

> Management responsibility: Management should define and document a quality policy, an organisation structure, including responsibility and authority. Management should make available verification resources (inspectors), appoint a management representative and carry out management reviews.
>
> Quality system: The quality system must be documented, including a manual, procedures and work instructions.
>
> Inspection and test: Inspection should be performed on receipt of goods. Documented procedures should define the appropriate tests.
>
> Corrective action: A corrective action procedure must be documented, defining what is to be analysed, how corrective actions are to be initiated and obtained to prevent re-occurrence.
>
> Internal quality audits: These must be planned and scheduled to verify the effectiveness of the quality systems. Audits must be performed by staff independent of authority responsible for the area being audited. The procedures for audits, follow-up actions and reporting must be documented. (Seddon, 2000, pp 5-6; see also Chestnut, 1997)

The assumption is that most businesses will already have these procedures in place. However, they are unlikely to be as complete or systematic as the system required by ISO 9000. This is why accreditation involves several stages in which a company produces a plan with the aim of remedying the defects. This has created commercial opportunities for consultants who hold workshops on how to register, and conduct dry-run inspections of quality systems and procedures.

As in the case of TQM, there is a critical literature, suggesting that the effort and expense expended on these programmes does not necessarily result in improved quality. TQM is sometimes criticised for only leading to short-term improvements to competitiveness or performance, since it is difficult to sustain the initial enthusiasm generated by liberation from established rules or procedures (Milakovich, 1995). The standards industry, by contrast, is accused of producing unnecessary and debilitating bureaucracy, through the amount of work required to obtain accreditation as a quality organisation, and then to audit and document quality systems. Seddon believes that compliance with ISO 9000 actually reduces quality:

> The evidence suggests that registration to ISO 9000 leads to sub-optimal performance. In simple terms, it makes performance worse. So many organisations have implemented ISO 9000 in such as way that it has added to costs, made customers unhappy, and demoralised staff; but most of all it has prevented organisations taking opportunities to improve performance which they might otherwise have seen.

> It is possible, and we would argue, predictable that ISO 9000 has inflicted damage to the competitive position of hundreds of thousands of organisations. It is all the more disturbing that this should have been done in the name of quality. (Seddon, 2000, pp 28-9).

The reason why companies register, according to this critic, has nothing to do with a desire to please customers by raising standards. They spend large amounts of time writing quality manuals, and conducting reviews, simply because this is a requirement to obtain government contracts.

The new public management

Although inspectorates and the BSI are important forms of quality regulation in Britain, they do not fully explain why all kinds of public sector organisations, ranging from social work departments to schools, have become centrally concerned with quality. Osborne and Gaebler (1993) suggest that the quality movement in America developed at a local level as agencies sought to free themselves from central controls, and overcome financial problems, by implementing ideas developed by Deming and his associates in industry. In Britain, the reform movement in government was initially imposed as a top-down ideological measure in response to financial problems at a national level. This has become known as the new public management.

There is a large literature in social policy, sociology and public administration that describes these changes in the nature of government during the 1980s (for example, Pollitt, 1990; Dean, 1999). For those interested in the perspective and actions of people working inside government, the most informative study is arguably Spencer Zifcak (1994), which reports his experiences in the Financial Management Unit (FMU) during the early 1980s, and the beginnings of what became the Next Steps initiative. This is an unusual study about the civil service, in that Zifcak became a participant observer who was effectively sponsored by the FMU. In addition to conducting formal interviews, he was able to gain a deeper understanding of the reform programme through employing the traditional ethnographer's skills of chatting to people informally and 'hanging about':

> Being part of the implementation means that I was constantly discussing with members the issues and problems that they faced. Some of my most important insights were obtained not through formal interviews but over lunch, at the office Christmas party, in fleeting conversations in the corridor, or on the way home on the underground. (Zifcak, 1994, p 198).

The study inevitably favours the FMU viewpoint, so we do not hear much from those opposed to the reforms. Like most studies about official organisations, it also only hints at the political battles taking place behind the scenes, and we are not given much detail on what took place at meetings or training seminars. Nevertheless, it contains a lot of detail on how civil servants understood what was happening during this period.

The economic context to the reforms was the growth of inflation during the 1970s, along with high unemployment and borrowing. When Margaret Thatcher achieved power in 1979, she was ideologically committed to the monetarist ideas being promoted by Milton Freidman and other American economists. The central principles of monetarism were that inflation could be kept down by reducing borrowing, even if unemployment rose, and both taxation and public spending reduced. Although Zifcak does not explain the relationship between politicians and civil servants in any detail, it would appear that some officials in the civil service had already become converts to monetarism. This policy resulted in a high level of unemployment for most of the 1980s, and the closure or contraction of many manufacturing industries. There was also a determined attempt to reduce government spending. This is often presented as a failure, since social security spending rose dramatically during this period (Wilding, 1992). Outside this area of expenditure, the Thatcher government had some success in reducing the size of the civil service, cutting programmes and making others more efficient.

The most important element of the public sector reforms implemented from the mid-1980s was the devolution of responsibility and financial autonomy from departments of state to the agencies that delivered services. Two examples are that the Benefits Agency became separate from the Department of Health and Social Security, and the Courts Service became independent from the Lord Chancellor's Department. These still, however, work in a financial and regulatory framework established by the government department, and are assessed through performance indicators (Carter et al, 1992). What became known as the Next Steps initiative was informed by similar objectives to the movement for more autonomy in America: service departments would be able to innovate, free of central regulation, and the devolved organisations expected to focus on customers.

The new administrative culture that developed during the 1980s placed great emphasis on evaluation and monitoring of performance. One of the first actions of Thatcher's government was to establish the Audit Commission in 1982 as an independent agency that had the mission of improving quality and value for money across government. It has published numerous reports evaluating the effectiveness of government programmes, and promoting management methods in the public sector.[5] The Conservative government also established the Chartermark Awards sponsored by the Cabinet Office. These reward excellence in the management of public sector organisations such as schools or hospitals, and were modelled on the Malcolm Bainbridge Award in America.

Although sometimes presented as a successful revolution introduced by Margaret Thatcher, it is important to remember that the changes did not take place overnight, and there was a good deal of resistance within government. Zifcak gives the impression that the managers of agencies delivering services were keenest, although devolution of control involved making hard bargains with departments, and the Treasury resisted the whole process. He describes how the initial hopes of evaluating policies, rather than simply programmes, 'ran aground' (Zifcak, 1994, p 62) in that only minor policies were selected for the pilot study. He also describes how traditional tactics used by civil servants for slowing reform were directed against the first attempt to implement 'block budgeting' in the early 1980s, an early attempt to devolve power:

> In summary, what happened in the first five years ... is that managers were given new responsibilities but were not provided with the requisite authority, technical capacity or incentives to exercise them. This was a most potent formula for disillusionment and delay. (Zifcak, 1994, p 60)

The popular 1980s' television comedy, *Yes, Minister*, portrayed the civil service as capable of effortlessly creating obstacles to delay the implementation of policies it disliked. In this case, administrative reforms, originally suggested in the 1968 Fulton Report, were only implemented by the 1990s. Although Thatcher was clearly important, Zifcak's account suggests that anonymous civil servants had pursued a reform agenda over many years to introduce practices from industry into government, and only finally succeeded when an older generation retired from key positions.[6]

Zifcak gives a taste of the way in which this kind of cultural and organisational change takes place, but is only concerned with one agency within the civil service. He makes one think, however, not simply about the hidden persuasive and political work that takes place in building this kind of movement,[7] but about the extraordinary, and possibly unanticipated, results of this 20-year revolution in government. In 1979, institutions like schools, hospitals and police forces did spend some time measuring performance, reporting to various outside bodies, and preparing for inspections. But this was nothing like the amount of time and effort spent on accountability today. Moreover, this is an industry that continues to grow, with new inspectorates being created and even more effort expended in monitoring and assuring quality.

The expansion of quality assurance

Since the 1980s, quality assurance has become central to the delivery of public services in the United Kingdom. This can be seen in the growing numbers employed in organisations such as the Audit Commission, and consultancy firms advising public sector organisations about quality. This work, however, takes place behind the scenes, and the public face of this new emphasis on quality was the formation of new inspectorates that waged high-profile campaigns against 'failing' organisations. A good example of what symbolic interactionists would call successful claims making (Spector and Kitsuse, 1977) was the inquiry into the deaths of children who had undergone heart surgery at Bristol Royal Infirmary. This resulted in the creation of a new inspectorate for the NHS despite many years of opposition to greater regulation by doctors.

The growth of an industry

When academic texts on quality assurance use the term 'industry', this can sound slightly pejorative: it gives the impression that this occupational group is seeking to advance its own interests, rather than serving the public like a profession. There are not, however, the same undertones when talking about 'the insurance industry' or 'financial services industry'. The reason probably lies in the fact that quality assurance is a relatively new occupation that is not liked by professionals.

The extent to which quality assurance has become either an industry or profession is debatable. To be an industry, one would expect to find large numbers of people working in quality assurance, selling a distinctive service or product. To be a profession, one would expect it to have developed a body of technical knowledge and expertise that is taught in specialist courses, and leads to accreditation by a professional association (Carr-Saunders and Wilson, 1933). Neither of these seems to fit and one can even question whether quality assurance is a separate occupation, rather than a sub-field within management or the civil service, or in the case of auditing, within accountancy. The problem is evident when one considers the range of organisations in which quality assurers are working. In Britain, these include the Audit Commission, numerous inspectorates, consultancy firms, accrediting bodies such as the BSI, government departments and the institutions providing services such as schools, police forces and hospitals.

The quality assurance industry is probably best understood as a loose network or community (Hood et al, 1999), where everyone draws on a common knowledge base and language that originates with American management theory. There is, however, no clear boundary between this and a range of administrative careers, so civil servants or senior managers in public sector organisations can join an inspectorate for a few years before moving to another administrative post. The extent to which the quality assurance industry has grown, and whether it will continue to expand or has reached a plateau, is difficult to establish. We do know, however, that the proportion of managerial and administrative jobs in advanced industrialised economies continues to rise, and part of this is due to the expansion of quality assurance.

The creation of new inspectorates

The internal politics of change within government departments and inspectorates are difficult to research. What does seem apparent, however, is that there were political pressures on departments to establish or strengthen this form of regulation, particularly during the 1990s. Ofsted was formed in 1992, partly out of dissatisfaction among Conservative politicians with Her Majesty's Inspectors of Schools, who were perceived as too soft on professionals (Fitz-Gibbon and Stephenson-Forster, 1999). The Quality Assurance Agency for higher education (QAA) was created in 1996. It took longer establishing or modernising other inspectorates. The Commission for Health Improvement (CHI) and Commission for Social Care Inspectorate (CSCI) that replaced the Social Services Inspectorate were established in 2004.

Whether coincidentally or otherwise, these new agencies were sometimes headed by charismatic leaders, such as Chris Woodhead, the second director of Ofsted, who pursued high-profile media campaigns against what were portrayed as 'failing' teachers. These took place in the context of attempts by government to introduce controversial reforms designed to improve national performance. A standard curriculum was introduced into schools, in which some minority subjects disappeared, and there was a much greater emphasis on tests (Woodhead, 1998). John Randall, the director of QAA, also regularly issued press statements criticising universities for not responding to the challenges created by expansion in 1992.

Unsurprisingly, Woodhead and Randall each met tremendous resistance in promoting these reforms. Woodhead resigned in 2000. Randall was forced out in 2002 when a powerful lobby of vice-chancellors in elite universities mobilised against him. Despite these controversies, both inspectorates have been successful in expanding their activities. This is partly because they have the political support of government ministers, but also because the system of monitoring quality through inspections has become institutionalised. There is much potentially to be lost, and little to be gained, through challenging this system of regulation.

The Bristol Royal Infirmary inquiry

The most recent example of the expansion of quality assurance is the creation of a new inspectorate for the National Health Service. It is again hard as an ordinary member of the public to gain access to the political struggles that took place in the Department of Health in establishing this new system of regulation, or the history of attempts to make the work of doctors accountable. Fortunately, in this case, there is a rich source of public information available in the report of the public inquiry into children's heart surgery at the Bristol Royal Infirmary (Kennedy et al, 2001).

This report is a 1,200-page document, with a further few thousand pages of annexes, in which one can read the evidence presented to the inquiry. It is partly an account of what happened at the Paediatric Cardiac Surgical Service at this hospital from 1984-95, with the objective of establishing why there was an unusually high death rate for children undergoing open heart surgery and why it took so long before this was recognised as a problem. It also contains recommendations for the formation of a new quality inspectorate, and other measures designed to improve the quality of medical work, including compulsory continuing education and accreditation, and periodic appraisals for senior managers. Whether or not this was the intention, the whole document can be read as a sustained argument for doctors and, by implication, other professionals to be subject to greater regulation.

According to the report, the reason for the high death rate at Bristol could not be attributed to the poor clinical skills of particular individuals, although it comes close to saying that the chief surgeon was not as competent as a specialist paediatric heart surgeon would have been in conducting these operations. Another possible cause that is discounted is the underfunding that prevented the trust from appointing a new surgeon or making other improvements, including increasing the number of trained nurses, providing an adequate number of cardiologists and surgeons, and ending the unsatisfactory provision of a service on a split site. Since every hospital suffered from underfunding, this in itself could not explain why Bristol had a lower performance.

The thrust of the argument is that the main failing at Bristol, and throughout the National Health Service, was that there was no proper system for monitoring quality. The chief surgeon, Mr Wisheart, was blamed not for clinical incompetence (although this was implied), but for a lack of 'insight' in failing to recognise that the high death rate was due not to the problems of patients, but to a system that had become inadequate, and for not listening to concerns raised within the hospital. The Chief Executive, Dr Roylance, was criticised for believing that it was 'impossible' for managers to interfere with consultants (Kennedy et al, 2000, p 68), and that his role should be 'to provide and co-ordinate the facilities which would allow the consultants to exercise clinical freedom'. By contrast, the hero in the report was Dr Bolsin, an anaesthetist who raised concerns repeatedly within the hospital, but was ignored and eventually became a whistleblower when a third party contacted the satirical magazine *Private Eye*. He was committed to improving quality through auditing, and had 'been elected the first National Audit Co-ordinator for the Association of Cardiothoracic Anaesthetists of Great Britain, responsible for the collation of data on outcomes in cardiac surgery on adults' (Kennedy et al, 2000, p 139).

The Chief Executive was also criticised for allowing a 'club culture' to develop, in which criticism was kept within the group. The surgeon and the rest of the medical team met at each other's houses to review quality, but the meetings were not minuted. The following paragraph reports the anaesthetist's version of what took place after one meeting:

> On 28 July 1991 an audit meeting was held jointly between the cardiologists, cardiac surgeons and anaesthetists. Dr. Bolsin drafted minutes, referring to a problem with mortality which he expressed as having been 'thought to be reaching crisis proportions', based on the differences between the figures in the Annual Reports and the national figures, but which had been averted. Dr. Bolsin said: 'I thought I was reflecting what the unit told me, but I was subsequently told after producing these minutes that they were not representative and I was not to produce them ever again'. (Kennedy et al, 2000, pp 138-9)

He was also allegedly told that 'these minutes will not be circulated, this is not how we do things, I do not want you keeping minutes again'. The Chief Executive's management style was described by various critics (who emerged in force during the inquiry) as 'giving rise to an "oral culture", in that he preferred to avoid setting things down in writing unless necessary' (Kennedy et al, 2000, p 68).

The underlying problem, according to the report, did not lie with the failings of individual doctors or managers, since the NHS as a whole had not sufficiently addressed the issue of quality. One learns, for example, that there had been a tradition in the Department of Health not to interfere with clinical autonomy. Change in the NHS only took place when general managers were introduced with experience from the private sector. Clinical audit was introduced in 1991, and required trusts to ensure that doctors met regularly to review performance. The following extract from the report, which is based on evidence given by the Chief Executive, suggests not only that this was inadequate, but that doctors resented these developments, and attempted to thwart the reforms:

> Notwithstanding the national endorsement of medical and then clinical audit, the approach adopted was educational. The aim was to encourage review. Audit was not seen as a tool systematically to identify problems or to monitor the outcome of care for all patients. As [the Chief Executive] put it, referring to the requirements placed on trusts in 1991: 'At that stage, it was simply required that there be audit activities in which every doctor participated and that general results be reported. Audit was still said to be primarily an educational activity: its monitoring potential was very much underplayed at this stage'. He also stated '… I was aware of a strong feeling within the medical profession that audit was going to be used as yet another management tool and I felt that its introduction … needed to be handled very carefully in order to encourage doctors to participate'. (Kennedy et al, 2000, p 88)

Although the report states that it is concerned with improving systems, as opposed to criticising groups or individuals, it is difficult to escape the conclusion that the main villain was the medical profession for resisting quality assurance. The recommendation was not simply that better training is required (for example, in 'communication skills') but also that there was a need for more systematic and effective regulation. It proposed that 'Continuing Professional Development (CPD), periodic appraisal and revalidation must be compulsory for all healthcare professionals' (Kennedy et al, 2000, final summary, p 15). It also proposed that clinical audit should become compulsory and that performance data be collected and made publicly available by health trusts. This would require establishing two new regulatory bodies: 'a new independent Council for the Regulation of Healthcare Professionals' that would be responsible for accreditation and 'report to the Department of Health and to Parliament'; and 'an independent overarching body, the Council for the Quality of Healthcare' that would coordinate and integrate the activities of existing bodies such as the National Institute for Clinical Excellence and the Commission for Health Improvement (Kennedy et al, 2000, final summary, p 15).

These recommendations did not, of course, simply reflect the views and expertise of the inquiry panel, but drew on expert evidence from quality assurers working for the Department of Health, who had been campaigning for similar changes over a period of years against opposition in the department and from the medical profession. One gets the sense of professional groups resisting this form of regulation successfully over many years, but equally so the determination of government to introduce management into the health service, and with it the practices of measuring and assuring quality advocated by American management theorists like Deming, and in Britain by the BSI. It is also apparent that the beneficiaries in this process are not simply patients, but the organisations established to measure and monitor quality, and more generally quality assurance as a new occupation.[8]

A site for sociological investigation

Writing a comprehensive history of quality assurance would be a difficult enterprise without having access to key informants or primary sources from government departments or the quality movement. This kind of change takes place gradually over many years, and involves a number of parallel developments. The influence of the quality movement in America on civil servants and politicians in Britain is clearly an important factor. One could even argue that, whenever a manager in a British school, hospital or police force uses a phrase like 'continuous improvement', 'benchmarking' or 'focusing on the customer', he or she owes an unacknowledged debt to charismatic Americans such as W. Edwards Deming.

Quality assurance may not seem immediately interesting as a site for sociological investigation since it involves mainly dry, technical work. With the exception of investigations into national scandals such as the Bristol Royal Infirmary inquiry, the numerous routine documents and reports about quality produced by public sector agencies and inspectorates have the character of technical reports written in colourless, bureaucratic language. Similarly, the many forms and procedures that have developed do not seem promising material for a sociological analysis (one colleague felt that a concentration on mundane detail would be simply 'too depressing'). Finally, some academic critics whose ideas are discussed in Chapter Seven have suggested that much of what takes place in auditing is ritualistic. If you accept this criticism, the reports and forms interest or engage bureaucrats and managers, but have little relevance to the actual problems that arise in delivering services. In the words of Erving Goffman (1967), perhaps 'the action' lies elsewhere.

Although quality regulation can seem like a dry and forbidding topic, this book aims to show that it is both important and interesting. It is important because everyone in the public sector, a major source of employment in post-industrial societies, is affected. It also allows one to revisit debates about the role of the professions and rationalisation that were first raised by classical sociologists in the 19th century, and are still highly relevant today. But it is also an interesting topic in the sense that, under the dull technical language, moral claims are made about professional competence and the delivery of public services.

Figure 2.1: Quality assurance in the British public sector

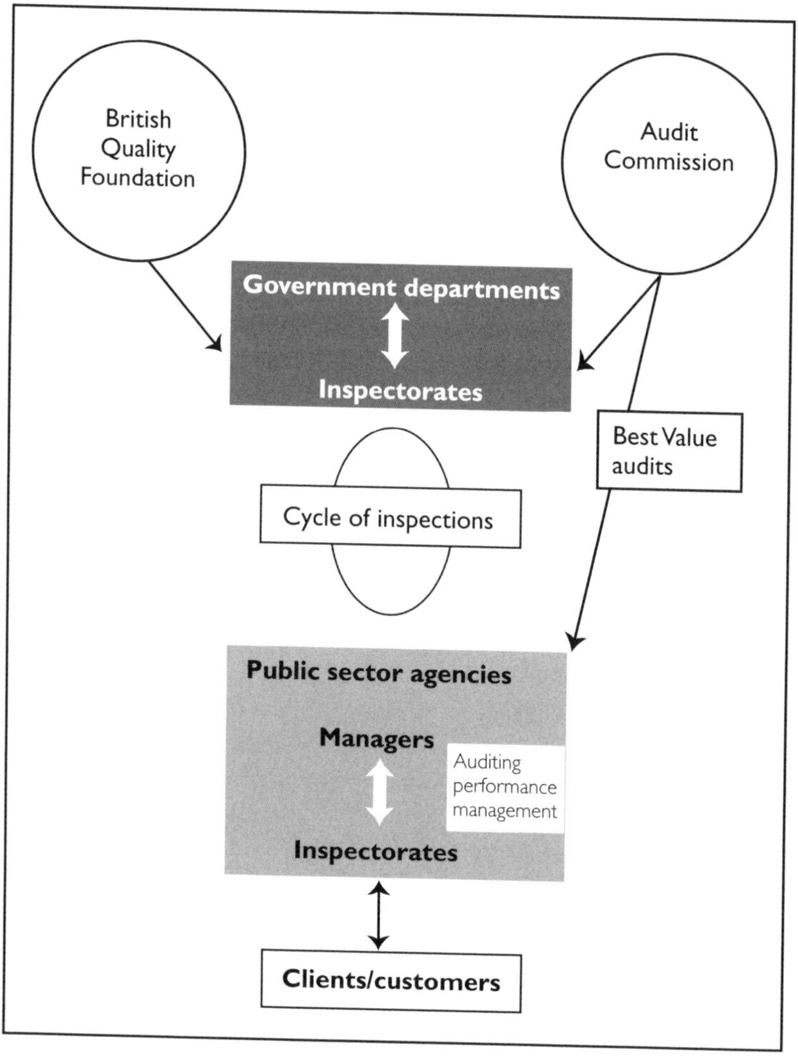

There has also been a significant shift in the way public sector workers such as doctors, teachers and university academics understand their work, and this deserves to be documented.

The main objective in this study is to consider and document the practical work involved at different levels of the diagram in Figure 2.1.

The next chapter looks at the work of professionals, and their relationship with clients at the base of the diagram. Chapter Four examines the perspective of government, and the work of auditors and inspectors. Chapter Five looks at the impact of regulation on managers and public sector organisations, and Chapter Six at how professionals experience and understand 'red tape'. Describing some aspects of these interlocking 'social worlds' (Strauss, 1993) also makes it possible to evaluate quality assurance as a form of regulation, and some critical perspectives are reviewed in the last chapter.

Notes

[1] Key texts include Deming (1986), Crosby (1979) and Peters and Waterman (1982).

[2] For a critical discussion of appraisals, see Grint (1995).

[3] See Bittner (1963) on radical social movements.

[4] There is a large literature on the new public management. See, for example, Pollitt (1993) and Walsh (1995).

[5] See, for example, Audit Commission (1992, 1993).

[6] Kuhn (1962) makes a similar point about scientific revolutions.

[7] Most social movements develop in the public sphere through a group organising public meetings, and seeking to generate support through the media or lobbying politicians or organisations (Klandermans and Staggenborg, 2002; Raeburn, 2004). This movement has a different character in that, as Zifcak reports, it grew through informal meetings between individuals seeking to make government more efficient and businesslike.

[8] Some idea of the expense involved is given by the Office of Public Services Reform (2003, p 15). Expenditure on the Commission for

Health Improvement 'rose from £1.5 million in set-up costs in 1999/2000 to £24 million in 2001/2'. Projected costs for the new Commission for Healthcare Audit and Inspection from 2002/03 were £50 million per year.

THREE

Professionals and quality

The ideal of professionalism
- Durkheim on professional ethics
- Expertise and democracy

The professions under attack
- The sociological critique
- The neo-liberal challenge

The nature of professional work
- Hughes on the professions
- An ethnomethodological perspective

How professionals understand quality
- The moral basis of professionalism
- The exercise of judgement

Why professionals object to quality assurance
- A question of trust
- A distrust of measurement

The high income and status enjoyed by traditional professional groups such as doctors and lawyers still make these attractive careers in which one finds a high proportion of people from upper-middle-class backgrounds. Workers in many other less highly remunerated occupations, such as nurses, teachers and social workers, as well as personnel officers, librarians and local government officers, have aspired to become professionals, and in doing so have improved their economic position and status relative to other groups. This means obtaining recognition from the rest of society as the custodians of a specialist body of knowledge and skills, and permission from the state to exercise the same control over who is entitled to hold a professional qualification (Freidson, 1970; Johnson, 1972; Larson, 1977; Abbott, 1988). Many writers have argued that the 20th century saw the triumph of professions as a form of organising work and expertise, but this dominance has been obtained at a price. The professions have always had admirers who believe that our whole society depends on having alternative sources of power and moral authority to the market or the state (Freidson, 2001). There are, however, also critics who see them as a self-interested group out to advance their own income and status at the expense of the public.

The objective in this chapter is to address the issue of how professionals understand quality, and why many have negative views about quality assurers.[1] However, to understand why this is such a charged issue, it is also necessary to revisit some of the general debates about professions and their place in society that have interested so many political commentators and social theorists in the last hundred years. Although some of these debates can become quite abstract, the various theoretical positions rest on widely shared prejudices about the role of experts in contemporary societies. A central issue is whether we should look up to occupations such as medicine, teaching and law, or regard them as interest groups that inflate the value of their services through monopolistic practices, and surrounding their activities in ritual and mystique. This arguably underpins the debates about accountability raised by the rise of quality assurance in public sector occupations. Should professions be allowed to regulate their own affairs, or do they need to be supervised by some outside agency representing the client or consumer?

Professionalism is a notoriously slippery and value-laden concept and, as Eliot Freidson (1994) has argued, the sociologist is often placed in the position of supporting the self-image of some powerful group, assisting other occupations that are on the make, or siding with state bureaucracies or corporations that have an ideological predisposition against professions. This is, however, familiar territory for any sociologist who writes about something that matters: it involves being drawn into, or taking sides in, political debates even though the protagonists often present them in other terms.

The chapter starts by reviewing the arguments of social theorists who believe that professions are beneficial for society, the criticisms made by left-wing sociologists during the 1960s and 1970s, and the successful ideological 'assault' by neo-liberal governments since the 1980s (Freidson, 2001, ch 8). None of these academic writers looks in much detail at what is involved in day-to-day practice or how professionals understand their own activities, and the next section considers the contribution made by the American interactionist sociologist Everett Hughes and ethnomethodologists in addressing these questions.

The rest of the chapter looks at two characteristics of professional work, drawing on an ethnographic study of a law firm, and the author's experience of working in higher education. The first is the moral basis of professionalism, so that practitioners often disagree with clients over how a service should be delivered. The second is the exercise of judgement, often in circumstances where there is no right or wrong answer on how to perform an occupational task. The chapter concludes with some observations on why professionals object to quality assurance. The argument is that, although there may be other reasons, occupational groups such as lawyers, doctors and teachers who have invested some effort in learning a set of skills, and who see themselves as serving the public, particularly object to the implication that they lack competence or cannot be trusted. They also believe that the measures employed by quality assurers cannot address the technical or moral content of their work.

The ideal of professionalism

This section revisits some of the classic statements of the professional ideal made by Emile Durkheim, Talcott Parsons and Carr-Saunders and Wilson. They all believed that professions benefited society as a source of moral authority and expertise. However, their arguments go rather further than this, and it is significant that they all promote strong independent professions as essential for democracy. Since the 20th century saw a rise in centralised state power, and most professionals today are employed by the state and are subject to increasing managerial control over the content of their work, it is timely to consider their views.

Durkheim on professional ethics

Although most of Durkheim's analysis of the problems experienced by complex industrialised societies have stood the test of time, and continue to influence many sociologists and political commentators, this cannot be said for his writings on the professions. As Durkheim himself admits, his proposal for what appears to be a return to the medieval guild 'comes up against historical prejudices that make it still repugnant to most' (Durkheim, 1959, p 13). This was true in his own times, and is certainly the case today when neo-liberal ideas about the need for cutting state regulation and containing public spending are again dominant. However, on closer inspection, he turns out, first, not to be concerned with what we would understand as the professions in the narrow sense of occupational groups with specialist technical expertise, such as doctors and lawyers. He is also arguing for a middle way between giving free reign to market forces and direct state control of the economy, which, despite the success of neo-liberalism as a political movement, still reflects how countries like Britain are currently governed.

Durkheim's starting point, like the other classical sociologists, was the social and psychological problems created by an economic system based on commodity production and the 'cash nexus', where there is no great satisfaction or fulfilment in work, and occupational specialisation creates conflict between managers and workers. His central argument in *The division of labour in society* (1984) is that industrialised societies are no longer held together by shared moral values. In his essay on professional ethics, he argues that the triumph of liberal economic principles (what we would today call 'neo-liberalism') in organising industry and commerce undermines the rest of society:

> If we follow no rule except that of clear self-interest, in the occupations that take up nearly the whole of our time, how should we acquire a taste for any disinterestedness, or selfishness or sacrifice? Let us see, then, how the unleashing of economic interests has been accompanied by a debasing of public morality. We find that the manufacturer, the merchant, the workman, the employee in carrying on his occupation, is aware of no influence set above him to check his egotism; he is aware of no moral discipline and so he scouts any discipline at all of this kind. (Durkheim, 1959, p 12)

Durkheim is not concerned here with occupations offering specialist services such as doctors or lawyers, but makes the wider point that there should be an ethical dimension to day-to-day work in factories and small businesses. He argues that ethics should arise within particular industries and be established by the state through corporations that devise and enforce occupational codes of conduct:

> There should be rules telling each of his workers his rights and duties, not vaguely in general terms but in precise detail, having in view the most ordinary day-to-day occurrences. All these various inter-relations cannot remain forever in a state of fluctuating balance. A system of ethics, however, is not to be improvised ... the true cure for the evil is to give the professional groups in the economic order a stability they do not so far possess. Whilst the craft union or corporate body is nowadays only a collection of

individuals who have no lasting ties with one another, it must become or return to being a well-defined and organized association. (Durkheim, 1959, p 13)

Durkheim did not explain in much detail what ethical principles guilds would promote in manufacturing industry, although he seemed to envisage that they could arbitrate in industrial disputes, and maintain standards of health and welfare that at that time lay outside state control. He was not, however, proposing direct regulation of the kind that already existed in the late 19th century and has subsequently massively expanded with the rise of the welfare state. Instead, he took the view that effective moral self-regulation, or standards of conduct, could not develop outside a cohesive group that met regularly, and was 'exercised' through routine activities in the workplace. Professional association (in this broad sense) could reach areas of public life and conduct unavailable to the state.

Durkheim gives examples of how this already operated from 'a number of the professions' that already formed organised groups. He notes how moral values can be specific to an occupation, so that 'it is the doctor's duty on occasion to lie', whereas this would not be ethical for a scientist, priest or soldier. If 'a whole group of workers' in manufacturing got together in regular meetings, facilitated by government, they would also develop shared values, and enforce 'common practices' (Durkheim, 1959, p 9). This would benefit society as a whole by restoring a sense of community and belonging, reducing industrial unrest, and combating the competitive individualism created by free market capitalism.

Although this might seem a naive response to the problem of inequality and industrial unrest in capitalist societies, it is interesting to consider that state regulation has effectively accomplished many of the reforms Durkheim was hoping would be established through self-regulating guilds. He was advocating what today would be described as third way capitalism, in which there is a balance between state and market (Giddens, 1994). He even has something interesting to say in this essay about how more regulation in manufacturing industry (which would presumably include meetings where workers and managers talk about quality) might create excessive bureaucracy:

In our own minds we see all regulation of this sort as a kind of policing, maybe vexatious, maybe endurable, and possibly calling forth some outward reaction from individuals, but making no appeal to the mind and without

> any root in the consciousness. It appears like some vast set
> of workshop regulations, far-reaching and framed in general
> terms: those who have to submit to them may obey in
> practice if they must, but they could not really want to
> have them. (Durkheim, 1959, p 28)

Durkheim goes on to defend himself against the charge from a sympathetic critic that this form of regulation will produce compliance without addressing the selfish, individualistic values that are the root of the problem in a capitalist economy. He is not, therefore, simply promoting the value of the professions, but arguing for a much wider form of community (or 'social solidarity') based on people coming together in voluntary associations to regulate their own activities. A new ethic of trust and cooperation that will eliminate strikes and industrial conflict can be encouraged and promoted by state action. The danger he anticipates is that an active or interventionist state, concerned with delivering a good quality of life, may produce 'some vast set of workshop regulations' that everyone must obey, but no one really wants.

Expertise and democracy

Another sociological theorist who expressed positive views about the professions was Talcott Parsons. He believed that experts would become increasingly important in an advanced industrial society:

> It seems evident that many of the most important features
> of our society are to a considerable extent dependent on
> the smooth functioning of the professions. Both the pursuit
> and the application of liberal learning are predominately
> carried out in a professional context. Their results have
> become so closely interwoven in the fabric of modern
> society that it is difficult to imagine how it could get along
> without basic structural changes if they were seriously
> impaired. (Parsons, 1949, p 34)

A claim made during the early 20th century by professional associations is that they were motivated by a desire to serve the public, rather than to make money. Parsons offered a sophisticated endorsement of this view, although he took care to distance himself from the arguments made by lay people. While he accepted that professions are motivated by an altruistic commitment to science rather than the pursuit of profit (Parsons, 1949), he argued that this contrast could be taken too far, since it was possible to benefit society and make money. He also recognised that the professions, government and industry have a lot in common, and are necessarily connected and mutually interdependent in all kinds of ways. They were each, for example, based on applying rational, technical competence to solve social problems. Parsons argued that this was a key development in the modern world, and far more significant than the fact that the three occupational groups appeared to be governed by different values.

Nevertheless, despite these and other qualifications, Parsons still offered a positive view of professions that implicitly accepts their claim to be motivated by a service ethic, and the benefits that doctors, lawyers and teachers offer to society. He also wrote sympathetically about the pressures placed on them as agents of social control or intermediaries between the state and the citizen, the moral and ethical dimensions of expertise, and the difficulties involved in interpreting a complex and evolving body of technical knowledge. Without making the point explicitly, he implied that the professions deserve their high status and income, and autonomy in their work. He even argued that they act as a positive, constraining force on business and the state (Parsons, 1968), and were likely to become even more important for a good society as the economy developed.

Carr-Saunders and Wilson (1933) advanced a similar argument in defence of the professions in England during the inter-war years. They saw their 'chief distinguishing characteristic' as 'the application of an intellectual technique to the ordinary business of life, acquired as the result of prolonged and specialised training' (Carr-Saunders and Wilson, 1933, p 492). They were impressed by the growing number of occupations in which practitioners received this training, and professional associations determined whether one could practice. These included established professions such as law and medicine but also professionalising occupations such as pharmacy, nursing, chemistry and architecture. They predicted that professions would become increasingly common in economic life. Management would become a profession and, eventually, even those 'engaged either in routine intellectual occupations or in manual labour' would belong to 'vocational associations' (Carr-Saunders and Wilson, 1933, p 493). This is because, as science advanced, all work would require abstract knowledge:

> In the long run, technical advance implies an increase in
> the number of those doing more or less specialized

intellectual work relative to the number of those who are engaged in manual labour or in unspecialised intellectual routine. It may be that, while the extension of professionalism upwards and outwards may be fairly rapid, its extension downwards, though gradual and almost imperceptible, will be continuous. Thus, taking the long view, the extension of professionalism over the whole field seems in the end not impossible. (Carr-Saunders and Wilson, 1933, pp 493-4)

As well as believing that the rise of the professions was inevitable, they argued that it would be beneficial. They suggested, to begin with, that governments should take heed of expert knowledge. This argument for 'knowledge in the service of power' can be contrasted with the suspicion of theorists like Weber and Foucault towards the Enlightenment belief that every social problem can be solved through the application of science and reason. Professions were also presented in almost Burkean terms as traditional groups that protect society against violent social upheaval. They were not, however, simply concerned about the possibility of a socialist revolution, but of the problems that 19th-century writers like De Tocqueville (2003) and Michels (1959) had identified in liberal democracies. A central theme was the growing power of large organisations such as state bureaucracies and large corporations that have reduced individual freedom:

> Owing to the growth in the size of communities, the increasing complexity of organization, the appearance of huge corporations, and the employment by the State of its powers of direction, the individual member of the community feels helpless. He works under direction, and there is little to arouse his sense of responsibility; the air is heavy with oppression in the face of which he is apathetic unless roused into uninformed and violent protest. These protests may take the form of attacks against capitalism and other imaginary systems, but they are seldom or never directed against the very obvious chains which bind men down with ever increasing success. (Carr-Saunders and Wilson, 1933, p 500)

In this increasingly regulated society, they argued that belonging to a profession offers the only opportunity for individuals to obtain a measure of 'freedom' and 'dignity' in working for large organisations.

They offer an alternative set of values that can ensure social stability in the face of the growth of the state and market, and goes against the fads and fashions spread by the media. Unfortunately, they did not give much detail about the relationship between professionals and the state, or anticipate tensions between them. They did, however, argue for extending the welfare state, so all citizens could benefit from professional expertise.

The professions under attack

The ascendancy of the professions lasted up to the 1960s. Since then they have increasingly come under attack. The intellectual arguments against professions were initially advanced by sociologists, particularly Weberians and interactionists, who debunked their claim to specialist expertise and status. Neo-liberal governments since the 1980s have also pursued a successful campaign against professionals as a privileged occupational group, both through feeding negative stories to the media and making them subject to regulation by independent inspectorates. It is ironic that progressive critics who argued for greater regulation of doctors and lawyers in the 1970s are now themselves subject to the same regulation.

The sociological critique

The idea that professionals are motivated by altruism and can be trusted to run their own affairs and safeguard democracy has been attacked by many social theorists and commentators. Few go as far as Ivan Illich (1973), who argued that specialist training for many expert jobs is unnecessary, and that the same services could be delivered by lay people. It is, however, generally agreed by most liberal commentators that, far from being altruistic, professions seek to increase their own earning power by securing a monopoly on accreditation. An early example of this cynical view of the professions can be found in Weber's (1991) portrayal of society as a site for struggle between different occupational groups seeking to secure economic advantage and higher status, through practices of exclusion or social closure.

Many sociological studies have drawn on historical case studies to show how professions have secured a position of dominance through securing a favourable relationship with the state, so that they can exclude competitors who offer the same services at lower rates to the consumer (Johnson, 1972; Larson, 1977). This is quite a dry and forbidding literature, and there are many technical disputes over how this happened in different occupations, and between different analytic models of professionalisation. In simple terms, however, the critique debunks claims for the altruism of the professions. From this perspective, the long years of training required to become a doctor, lawyer or accountant have less to do with the skills and knowledge needed in the job than with the need to limit entry and so raise professional incomes. Occupations in which one does not need extensive training also have an incentive to professionalise by inventing new fields of technical expertise, and sometimes new languages that are taught on professional courses. These occupations include teachers, nurses and social workers, but also managers and counsellors. In broader terms, our whole society is based on credentialism, which means one has to spend increasingly long periods in formal education in order to compete in the labour market (Collins, 1979).

Elliot Freidson argues that any group aspiring to become a profession must secure 'autonomy' or 'control over the content and terms of work' (Freidson, 1970, p 134). This also explains why professions develop codes of ethics that do not exist in trade or craft occupations:

> ... a code of ethics or some other publicly waved banner of good intentions may be seen as a formal method of declaring to all that the occupation can be trusted, and so of persuading society to grant the special status of autonomy. The very existence of such a code implies that individual members have the personal qualities of professionalism, the imputation of which is also useful for obtaining autonomy. (Freidson, 1970, p 135)

This unflattering view of the professions was promoted with some energy by neo-Weberian researchers during the 1960s and 1970s, and also by interactionists, to the extent that it still informs most sociological writing on the professions. There are different strands in interactionism (as in any sociological tradition) and the next section shows that at least some of the best studies have not been motivated by a debunking or critical intent. Nevertheless, the idea that there was a 'backstage' area in every institution hidden from public view in which potentially disreputable activities occurred, or that profession should be regarded as a lay or 'folk' concept, rather than having any scientific value, were intended to offend the establishment. For this reason, Erving Goffman's (1961) *Asylums* remains an important book that encourages critical thinking about what happens behind closed doors in public sector institutions.

Moreover, one should not forget Marxist and feminist sociologists, whose ideas were popular and influential during the 1970s and 1980s, and still inform critical thinking in universities even though they are usually combined and cross-fertilised in exotic ways with poststructuralist thought and political ideas from other progressive intellectual movements such as environmentalism, queer and critical race theory. From a Marxist perspective, professions were often seen as a tool of dominant groups in society, or as agents of social control through the criminal justice system and welfare state (Larson, 1977). From a feminist perspective, they were bastions of male privilege that systematically excluded and promoted sexist views about women (Witz, 1992). Neither of these arguments is much heard today, although it would be hard to argue that class and gender are no longer relevant categories for understanding the distribution of income, wealth or occupational opportunities in industrialised societies.

The neo-liberal challenge

Sociology, as it is currently taught in universities, has been mostly shaped by the generation that entered academic life during the expansion of universities that took place in the 1960s. It developed in Britain as part of a larger cultural and political movement that achieved substantial reforms, through the political process, that benefited minority groups and the working class. In America, sociologists participated in the anti-war movement and campaigns for civil rights, and were criticised for promoting a relativist tolerance towards 'deviant' groups. In this sort of progressive climate, it is easy to see why sociologists were critical towards the professions, and the public was receptive to these ideas. One important development was that newspapers and television news started to report on professions, and 'the establishment', with less deference; even today there are regular exposés of failings in hospitals, social services and the criminal justice system, and of misconduct by professionals, that would not have been possible during the 1950s.

The hopes of progressives for radical change during the 1970s turned out to be short-lived, and there has been a political shift towards the right across the developed world, and the election of governments committed to economic liberalism. This means reducing taxation, accepting a higher level of economic inequality, encouraging enterprise and competition, attempting to reduce state expenditure and borrowing, and reducing trade barriers. Margaret Thatcher's government in Britain, which won three elections during the 1980s, reformed the civil service and tried to reduce the power of the professions. During the Thatcher government, the miners were not the only 'enemies within'. There was also the state-funded BBC, the Church of England, the judiciary, lawyers, universities and the medical profession, all of which were accused of obstructing necessary change, or engaging in exclusionary practices designed to maintain artificially high incomes. The New Labour government led by Tony Blair has also criticised these occupational groups (Marquand, 2004).[2]

Although there are some similarities between the critiques of professions made by 1960s' progressive sociologists and neo-liberal governments since the 1980s, there are also important differences. Progressives have always enjoyed critique for its own sake, and have a preference for utopian solutions (such as the Marxist dream that, after the revolution, the state would 'wither away', so presumably there would be no need for professions). Neo-liberals, on the other hand, have a well-thought-out political agenda, and have not simply engaged in a war of words against the professions, but have also significantly changed key institutions in British society. Hospitals, universities and the legal profession have been substantially restructured to pursue neo-liberal goals through changing how they are funded and creating internal markets and competition. Ironically, the earlier sociological critique of professional dominance may have prepared the ground for policies that critics believe will result in a two-tier system where people with money can obtain a better level of services.

The nature of professional work

The difficulty with most sociological writing on the professions is that it approaches the issues at a high level of abstraction. The most formidable pieces of scholarship in recent times, Andrew Abbott's (1988) *The system of professions* and Stephen Brint's (1994) *In an age of experts*, draw on empirical research to advance their theoretical arguments, but we learn very little in either study about what professionals do in occupational settings such as schools or hospitals, or how they understand their own activities.

The only real exceptions in sociology have been the interpretive traditions of interactionism and ethnomethodology, which have conducted ethnographic studies about professional practice. A key principle in each tradition is not to take official definitions at face value but to look at what actually happens in practice, and how the various occupations working in a particular institutional setting understand their own activities. Everett Hughes' (1971) writings address general themes, such as how occupations professionalise and the inevitable tensions that arise between professionals and clients, often drawing on interviews conducted by his postgraduate students as illustrative examples. Ethnomethodological studies have described what happens in professional practice, and suggest ways in which one can understand the nature of skill and competence.

Hughes on the professions

Although he did not hold himself out as a great theorist, and like other interactionists only saw himself as making modest generalisations based on what anyone could observe taking place in society, Everett Hughes has left a set of ideas and concepts that can take us a long way in understanding the professions. To begin with, there are his observations on what follows from having a licence or mandate to provide a particular service:

> Professionals profess. They profess to know better than others the nature of certain matters, and to know better than their clients what ails them or their affairs. This is the essence of the professional idea and the professional claim. From it flow many consequences....

> Since the professional does profess, he asks that he be trusted. The client is not a true judge of the value of the service he receives; furthermore, the problems and affairs of men are such that the best of professional advice and action will not always solve them.... The client is to trust the professional; he must tell him all secrets which bear upon the affairs in hand. He must trust his judgment and skill. In return, the professional asks protection from any unfortunate consequences of his professional actions; he and his fellows make it very difficult for anyone outside – even civil courts – to pass judgement upon one of their number. Only the professional can say when his colleague makes a mistake. (Hughes, 1971, pp 375-6)

This goes beyond the Weberian concept of social closure by identifying a set of tensions that arise even if an occupation is successful at professionalising. Hughes noted that many clients, either individually or as organised groups, attempt to influence how professionals deliver a service. However, even if professionals succumb to these pressures, there will always be an inherent tension built into the relationship. One example is that what for the professional is a routine event often has the character of an emergency for the client (Hughes, 1971, p 346). Hughes noted that the professional always has to upset some people by refusing to take on their problems, or not treating them as matters of serious concern.

Hughes also made some interesting observations about the reluctance of professionals to admit to making mistakes. A piece of research conducted by one of his students indicated that members of the public during the 1950s expressed absolute trust in their doctors and lawyers, in a way one would not find today. Similarly, professionals never criticised colleagues:

> The colleague-group will consider that it alone fully understands the technical contingencies, and that it should therefore be given the sole right to say when a mistake has been made. The layman, they may contend, cannot even at best fully understand the contingencies. This attitude may be extended to complete silence concerning mistakes of a member of the colleague-group, because the very discussion before a larger audience may imply the right of a layman to make a judgement; and it is the right to make the judgement that is most jealously guarded. (Hughes, 1971, p 320)

Although Hughes never directly criticised the professions, this passage suggests that he was sceptical about their claims always to know better than clients. Nevertheless, he also recognised that there are no easy solutions to the problem of providing an 'esoteric' service where 'the client is not in a position to judge for himself the quality of the service he receives' (Hughes, 1971, p 361).

An ethnomethodological perspective

One shortcoming of the sociological literature on the professions, including the research conducted by interactionists, is that it never looks at what practitioners do at any level of detail. This is partly because relatively few sociologists have a serious interest in what happens in doctors' surgeries, in classrooms or social work departments, or what in mainstream sociology is often called the 'micro-level' of society. Even if one wanted to do so, it requires considerable time and effort to understand day-to-day work in institutions such as schools or hospitals. In the first place, one needs permission to spend a long period of time in an organisation delivering a professional service, so that one not only gets to see routine tasks, but also starts to see them from the perspective of the people delivering the service. This requires not simply interviewing and observing practitioners as they meet clients and produce or interpret different kinds of texts, but also becoming familiar with how they discuss their work among themselves, both at formal meetings, and informally outside work.

One sociological tradition that has studied the social organisation of work in more detail is ethnomethodology, which is concerned with the practical content of day-to-day activities (Garfinkel, 1984, 2002). In contrast to studies about the labour process that draw mainly on interviewing (for example, Cohen et al, 2005; Cooke, 2006), ethnomethodologists have a commitment to participant observation in the strong sense of observing practitioners closely over a long period of time, and ideally developing a basic competence in some practical skill.[3] This has resulted in studies about the work of a number of occupations, including the police, scientists, lawyers, coroners, entrepreneurs and accountants, and more recently software designers and air-traffic controllers.[4] There is also a larger body of conversation analytic work that looks at how professionals use talk to accomplish their work based on the analysis of tape-recordings of classroom lessons or doctor–patient consultations. The analysis of even a short piece of conversation, such as a medical consultation, also reveals the difference in perspective between professionals and their clients (for example, Maynard, 2003).

Ethnomethodological studies about legal practice demonstrate how professional work always involves some degree of interpretation and judgement, so the police have to decide whether a youth they have arrested is a delinquent or needs psychiatric treatment (Cicourel, 1976), coroners must decide whether a death was accidental or a suicide (Garfinkel, 1997), and defence lawyers whether it is appropriate to offer plea-bargaining (Sudnow, 1965). The best studies also reveal something about the practical character of work, in the sense of how it usually involves working with limited resources and time, and doing the best one can in these circumstances. Practitioners also often have to juggle competing demands, and, in pursuing goals, respond creatively to unexpected events that threaten to disrupt a course of action (Cuff et al, 2006, p 158). In his study of a coroner's office, Garfinkel (1997) notes that outcomes can be retrospectively interpreted so that what is initially considered 'good work' may come to be seen as inadequate if someone complains. These can be understood as scientific findings, but also in a Wittgensteinian sense, as features of our everyday lives and social practices that we already know about and take for granted, but are not usually addressed in sociological studies about the professions.

How professionals understand quality

Ethnomethodologists see a value in investigating what happens in a particular social setting without having to address some wider theoretical or political question: they argue that this prevents you from seeing what actually happens in social settings, and how social activities are organised. Nevertheless, the findings made in their studies, or which one can obtain by looking at the world around you from this perspective, are often relevant to themes and questions in what Harold Garfinkel (2002) calls the 'formal' or 'analytic' literatures of mainstream social science. This section discusses two examples to draw out some features of professional practice: the work of criminal lawyers; and of lecturers in higher education. These case studies illustrate what Hughes means by the moral basis of professionalism, and what is involved in exercising professional judgement.

The moral basis of professionalism

According to Hughes (1971), professionals working in any organisation believe not only that they know more than clients by virtue of their training and knowledge, but also that they know what is in their best interests. When the author conducted an ethnographic study of a firm of criminal lawyers (Travers, 1997), this was a central finding. A one-hour episode of legal work, described in some detail in that study, involved a lawyer persuading a frightened and vulnerable client charged with shoplifting and assaulting a police officer to plead guilty. The client initially disputed the charges, but at the end of the interview pleaded guilty to both charges. Although the work involved and the reasoning behind the lawyer's approach were quite complex, a key factor was the lawyer's belief that, for this client, it was better to have the matter dealt with quickly than to put the client 'through the grief of a trial'. There are other examples in the study of how lawyers persuade defendants charged with more serious charges to accept professional advice. Here, for example, is an exchange between a youth charged with armed robbery during a conference with his barrister (Travers, 1997, pp 79-80), in which the barrister used the author's presence as a member of his legal team to exert additional pressure on a client:

1	S:	Now there's the statement of George Brown on page
2		190 of the deps.
3		[The barrister read out the statement. It was the
4		statement of a police officer who had seen Marks
5		entering a certain house on a particular date.]
6	C:	I'm not disputing he saw me. I'm disputing why he
7		did nothing about it.
8	B:	[closed eyes ... long pause] The reason I'm silent is
9		because I'm giving the matter careful thought. It's
10		not that I'm going to sleep.
11	C:	That's all right.
12	B:	[The barrister asked the client a few questions to
13		clarify some related facts] ... It's a dangerous
14		business Mr. Marks and I'll tell you why. What
15		happens is you ask the officer, did he know you were
16		wanted for robbery at the time. You were, weren't
17		you?
18	C:	Yes.
19	B:	You have a point to make. It's a dangerous point,
20		if there isn't other evidence that you're wanted
21		for it. How do we know how he knew you were
22		wanted for it? That's why it's dangerous. He
23		might say anything at all. He might say the police
24		back at the station had inadmissible evidence for
25		his behaviour.
26	C:	If I was wanted and then I raided a house, surely he
27		should have arrested me?
28	B:	Yes. But I'm interested in proving your innocence
29		[pause]. As I mentioned to you when we met in the
30		magistrates' court, you're going to have to keep
31		your eye on the ball. If we start making
32		peripheral points, that why does a police officer,
33		at the time you're wanted, not go chasing after you
34		with his blue light flashing, how does that prove if
35		you're innocent or guilty? It just distracts the
36		jury [pause] ... How many own goals do you want
37		me to score? [pause] Do you agree Helen? [She
38		nodded her head] Do you agree? [This was directed
39		to Marks who still looked doubtful. The barrister then
40		looked at me] Do you agree? [I murmured yes]. Do
41		you agree?

42		[The barrister again looked at the client]. You're the
43		boss you know. We're just here to help you.
44	C:	I just want to know when that Datsun was stolen.

Lawyers working in this firm and the barristers they instructed knew that, in cases of serious disagreement, clients could obtain advice and representation elsewhere. However, this did not stop them from giving what they saw as good professional advice. This is because as professionals they understood the craft of representing defendants in highly moral terms. The firm's charismatic owner, Jane Gregson, regularly complained about the 'uncaring' attitude of other firms, and the fact they would take cases to trial when this was not in the best interests of clients or, alternatively, were not sufficiently aggressive towards the police or magistrates in representing defendants. Critics of the firm argued that this was simply a sales pitch that should not be taken at face value, and that Gregson was providing a poor service by deliberately antagonising the police and magistrates. Whichever side one takes in this debate, the fact that there were different views, and that these were forcefully expressed, demonstrates that professionalism involves professing to know more than other professionals as well as more than the clients.

In higher education, one also finds that lecturers profess to know what is in the best interests of their students, and indeed the university degree can be seen as an exercise in moral education as much as learning about different academic disciplines. Many students take their studies seriously, engage with difficult material, and improve their writing and communication skills substantially before they graduate. Lecturers still, however, complain that some students do not have the skills or motivation to benefit, or coast through their studies with minimum effort. This has probably always been the case, although the pressure on teachers to reduce standards, or to entertain rather than cover difficult conceptual material, has become greater since governments in developed countries are committed to increasing student numbers.[5]

The key debate today is, therefore, between those who believe that academic standards and teaching methods should be preserved, and those who believe that universities should address the needs of 'non-traditional students'. There are still lecturers who have resisted using overhead slides or giving out lecture notes on the grounds that this encourages a passive form of learning. Many, however, embrace a new form of designing and delivering courses in higher education that has many similarities to schoolteaching. This attempts to engage students, at least in the early stages of a degree, with a variety of mostly undemanding tasks and exercises, and has significantly reduced the amount they are expected to write through such innovations as the short-answer or multiple-choice examination. As in the case of legal practice, one finds that there are different views on the purpose of education, and the extent to which professionals should respond to pressure from clients.

The exercise of judgement

A feature of professional work that has particularly interested ethnomethodologists is how it involves interpretation and judgement. A lawyer might have to decide, for example, whether a client has a strong or weak legal case, which depends on an evaluation of law and evidence. All kinds of tactical considerations are involved in presenting a case, deciding which procedures and legal arguments to use and, in the specialised craft of the trial, how to conduct effective examination and cross-examination of witnesses. A job well done involves a favourable outcome for the client, or the best that can be achieved given the circumstances, which is also a matter for judgement.

Describing what people do at work is difficult, and it is even harder trying to identify what is involved in doing competent and skilful work. Part of the difficulty is that experienced practitioners do not need to reflect on their activities, and there is usually no time for this. This comes across in the one-hour episode of work observed in which Gregson persuaded a vulnerable client to plead guilty. An analysis of this demonstrates that, whether or not one agrees with her handling of this case, a great deal of skill and judgement was involved. To begin with, she persuaded the defendant to plead guilty to the lesser charge and then attempted to persuade the prosecutor to drop the more serious charge. When this was unsuccessful, she persuaded the client to plead guilty, but to a version of events in which she was less culpable, and during the hearing she persuaded the magistrates and prosecutor (who had to telephone for instructions) to accept that one can commit a 'technical' theft.

The author was able to record in some detail what happened, and by interviewing the lawyer after the event, attempt to understand some of the issues. One judgement that Gregson made immediately was that this was a frightened and vulnerable defendant who would not benefit from a trial. She also came to the view, while 'taking instructions', that the client had committed the offence. It is entirely possible that another lawyer might have believed her version of events, and decided to fight the case: but there is no way of telling for sure, in this case, what was correct or moral. This is as good an example as any of the subjective nature of professional judgement.

One can make a similar point in relation to teaching in higher education. It should be no great cause for surprise that lecturers can disagree substantially on what makes a good piece of work. They may have different expectations about how essays should be structured and referenced, and whether a reasonable level of understanding can compensate for poor written English. They might also, however, disagree on what points need to be covered in answering a question, or even, in a subject like sociology, respond differently according to the political sentiments expressed. In some universities, elaborate systems have been established in which departments are asked to agree on marking criteria, and work is second marked, or sent to an external examiner in the event of disagreement. Since a subjective judgement is involved, there can be no scientific means of resolving these disputes. A common practice is for two markers who disagree to split the difference, provided this does not affect the classification, so that second marking becomes almost a ritual exercise. Understandably, teaching staff feel strongly about these issues, especially when it comes to assessing dissertations or PhD theses. Exercising judgement about quality is an important part of professional practice.

Why professionals object to quality assurance

The rest of this book is concerned with describing different quality assurance initiatives and their effect on public sector organisations and professionals. Chapter Six will review the complaints that groups such as doctors, teachers, lawyers, police officers and university lecturers make about quality assurance, including the fact that it results in burdensome and unnecessary 'red tape'. One does not, however, need to conduct empirical research to recognise why professionals object to quality assurance. This is because even the idea that outsiders are needed to regulate professional work undermines the status and independence of the professions. It also delivers the insulting message that professionals, despite professing to act in the best interests of the client, cannot be trusted to do so; and it suggests that the complex and subjective judgements that constitute professional work can be measured and evaluated using scientific methods.

A question of trust

Quality assurance originated in the quality movement in American manufacturing and the economic pressures faced by governments in the 1980s to improve the efficiency of public services. However, another important factor behind the success of this movement is the fact that since the 1960s the public has become less deferential towards experts and established institutions. There is widespread concern, fuelled by scandals reported in the media, that many professionals are not doing their jobs effectively. Although written in measured language, the report of the Bristol Royal Infirmary inquiry implied that many surgeons are incompetent, and that a culture of secrecy prevents mistakes from being acknowledged or addressed. Similarly, Chris Woodhead, during his time as Chief Inspector of Ofsted, was highly critical of failing teachers. More generally, the existence of any form of regulation implies that there must be incompetence and misconduct.

Given that the whole basis of professionalism is a claim to high moral standards, and the exclusive right to know what will benefit the public, it might seem surprising that professional associations have not campaigned more vigorously against greater regulation. The Law Society complained when the Conservative government removed its monopoly over conveyancing in the 1980s, which has forced many solicitors into other areas of work. The Bar Council complained when the government introduced legislation to remove its monopoly on advocacy in the higher courts. The teaching unions initially resisted the introduction of the national curriculum, which greatly increased workloads as well as reducing their independence and discretion. However, one does not find outrage expressed about the growth of quality assurance, or any movement of boycott or non-cooperation among professional groups.

One reason for this may be that professions have been in a weakened position for some time. When Carr-Saunders and Wilson were writing, professionals could dictate their own conditions in state employment. The rise in their numbers, partly due to the expansion of universities since the 1960s, has reduced this bargaining power. Professionals have also suffered from the successful case made by sociologists and other critics: that they principally exist to make money through exploiting an artificially scarce resource. Then there are the many scandals particularly in health and policing that have undermined their image of trustworthiness and competence. Many professionals resent quality assurance because it institutionalises this mistrust, even though it would like to be seen as complementing or strengthening self-regulation.

A distrust of measurement

The second reason why professionals might be expected to dislike quality assurance is because it requires having to measure performance using some objective standard. The next two chapters examine how auditors and inspectors understand the issue of measurement in more detail, and the practical work involved in producing league tables that compare different institutions. Before doing so, however, it is worth considering the issue of measurement as a conceptual problem.

Since professional work involves the exercise of situated judgement, it is impossible to devise a means of objectively assessing the quality of performance. If one wanted to measure and improve the quality of delivering a professional service, it would require agreeing on standards one could use as a benchmark. Using the example of the legal interview above, this would mean that when a lawyer persuaded a client to plead guilty it would be possible for an outsider, perhaps using a checklist, to decide if she or he had handled the case correctly. The difficulty for the quality assurer lies in the fact that two lawyers might disagree professionally on what was the right course of action given this particular set of circumstances. In this case, the lawyer believed that it would be cruel and unnecessary to subject a vulnerable client to 'the grief of a trial'. Another lawyer might have felt that the client's instructions should have been respected.

The assessment of competence becomes even more complicated when one realises that how one understands the evidence in any case is also a matter of interpretation and judgement. In the example above, the lawyer believed that the client had committed the offence, and so persuaded her to plead guilty. Another lawyer might have evaluated the evidence differently. Finally, there was the issue of interpreting the law. The lawyer sought to persuade the magistrates and prosecutor to accept a technical interpretation of the law of theft, so that the client could admit to playing a minor role in the offence. It would be difficult for an independent assessor, even with a legal background, to assess whether this was a correct reading of the law of theft, given that this is subject to different interpretations. In short, whether or not the lawyer behaved competently on this occasion, whether or not it was good-quality work, is a matter of professional judgement (Travers, 1994).

Exactly the same issues can be raised about how academics design courses, deliver lectures or mark essays. There are different ways of approaching the design and delivery of a course, and different criteria one can use in assessment. Outside sharing experiences on training courses, academics rarely have the time or show much interest in attending each other's lectures, and almost never criticise colleagues for poor teaching. One reason for this is that everyone agrees that there are different, but equally valid, ways of delivering courses. It is also accepted that two markers can differ considerably about the merits of an essay. Devising an objective standard, and trying to measure this, makes little sense in a professional field where practitioners cannot agree on what constitutes good performance. Quality assurers are, of course, well aware of this problem, and, instead of seeking to measure performance, restrict themselves to identifying indicators that can be used to make inferences about, or stand as proxies for, performance. In the case of law firms, one indicator favoured by the Legal Services Commission is whether files are neat and well-kept.[6] A proxy measure used by inspectors sent to observe university teaching in Britain during the 1990s was whether or not a lecturer made effective use of overhead slides, or was projecting to the back of a lecture hall sufficiently clearly. Inspection in each of these professional fields is now primarily based on examining general systems and policies, as opposed to actual performance, partly because of the interpretive problems created for inspectors of observing people at work.

Many lawyers and teachers resent these procedures not simply on the grounds that they imply a lack of trust, but also because they believe that it is impossible to measure professional competence in the same way as the quality of a manufactured product. Quality assurance, from this perspective, seems destined to become an empty ritual (the charge made by Power, 1997), since it cannot address how professionals understand their own work.

Notes

[1] For some examples, see Chapter Six.

[2] Neo-liberal governments dislike the professions on ideological grounds as privileged occupational groups. However, they also dislike them since professionals are considered to be politically liberal (Gouldner, 1979; cf Brint, 1994). This explains campaigns against the BBC for alleged left-wing bias, or against judges for protecting human rights.

[3] Garfinkel and Wieder (1991) call this 'the unique adequacy requirement of methods'.

[4] For a recent introduction, see Francis and Hester (2004).

[5] For an argument against the expansion of higher education, see Furedi (2004).

[6] When the Legal Aid Board (the predecessor of the Legal Services Commission) first considered how to measure quality, it attempted to establish objective standards for each type of case that auditors could look for on files, known as transaction criteria. For a critique of this procedure, see Travers (1994).

FOUR

Audit and inspection

A revolution in government
- Economic change
- The implications for business
- The rationale for public sector reform

Mechanisms of accountability
- Performance indicators
- Auditing
- Inspection
- Evaluation

The work of inspectorates
- Studying inspectorates
- Methodologies of inspection
- Making quality judgements
- The inspection visit
- The politics of inspection

The goal of continuous improvement
- Problems with audit and inspection
- Making the system work

The next two chapters examine how audit, inspection and evaluation have become central to the delivery of public services in the United Kingdom. This chapter is concerned with the perspective and work of government agencies concerned with quality assurance. Chapter Five looks at the effect on organisations like police forces, universities and hospitals that are subject to inspection, but also increasingly concerned with evaluating their own activities. In each case, there are already many histories of these administrative initiatives (for example, Pollitt, 1988, 1990; Walsh, 1991; Carter et al, 1992), and much technical discussion in the fields of public administration and management about the benefits of different regulatory models.[1] This literature is informative, since the authors are often insiders who are working in management positions. They often go beyond reading policy documents, which can be obtained in great quantities from the websites of different agencies, through interviewing policy makers about their own views.

Nevertheless, the focus is on constructing models, or evaluating the effectiveness of different management tools, rather than looking at the 'messy realities' (Stenson, 1998, p 350) of working life inside government agencies and departments.

From a sociological perspective, it seems important to examine the practical work involved both in developing policy, and putting it into practice (see Rock, 1994, 1995; Travers, 1999, ch 6). We can obtain a general understanding from an institutional history, or the consideration of ideal-typical management models, about how an organisation develops along with its objectives and achievements. However, one necessarily gets little sense of how managers and professionals get through their routine, day-to-day work, or how they encounter and solve problems in implementing or responding to some new government initiative. One also gets little sense of the culture of different organisations, or the personality of particular individuals, which is clearly vital in day-to-day work despite being treated as of no consequence in most academic disciplines outside the humanities. Finally, there is the question of how particular people understand success and failure, and the reasons for this, which means accepting there may be different viewpoints, and that these might change over time. This by no means exhausts what is practically involved in working in organisations (one cannot even specify what one will find in advance other than in the most general terms), but it points towards a different way of approaching this topic.

Ideally, one would want to spend a long time in one organisation for this kind of project, and get to know its problems and day-to-day work well. The overview of audit and inspection in this chapter is not based on this kind of access, and in fact the data presented are no different to those used by other studies: a few interviews with civil servants and inspectors and extracts from a few inspection reports. Nevertheless, if read in the right way, these materials can give some interesting glimpses into the practical character of work in different organisations that is not usually described in the existing literature on inspectorates or the new public management.[2] The chapter starts by looking at the view from government, focusing on the mechanisms that developed since the 1980s to monitor and assess quality. It then looks in more detail at the activities of inspectorates, which have taken on a more vigorous and interventionist role.

A revolution in government

Although an important part of their job requires communicating with the public, not least during election campaigns or at party conferences, most of the work of government ministers and their immediate circle of advisers remains hidden from the general public. The same could be said of other elite groups in society that have the ability to prevent outsiders from examining their routine activities in too much detail. There have not been any observational studies or fly-on-the-wall documentaries in mature democracies such as Britain about captains of industry, police chiefs, senior civil servants, university vice-chancellors, army top brass, senior judges, headmasters in public schools, the BBC upper echelons or newspaper editors, and information about how these groups make decisions is closely controlled.

One is, therefore, left with having to make the most of incomplete and potentially misleading sources: political autobiographies, often written to settle old scores, and which necessarily focus on individuals and a heroic view of politics; the occasional reflective account by journalists or other establishment insiders; and the public face of government presented to the public in parliamentary debates, White Papers and information given to the media. One can also, however, usefully draw on three things that everyone knows about the practice of politics, even though these are not usually acknowledged in public debate about policy issues. The first is that, these days, there is very little real difference in ideological terms between the main political parties, so the main objective is to demonstrate competence or managerial ability. The second is that no politician can be seen to be doing nothing: there always have to be new initiatives, or old policies dressed up in new language. The third is that, irrespective of the reform agendas of any political leaders, the problems facing any country inevitably have deep structural causes and persist over long periods of time.

In a mature industrialised country such as Britain, with a population of 60 million people, there are major social problems, such as crime, poverty and low levels of educational achievement, that resist any measures to reduce them. There are all kinds of institutions, inherited from the past, that cannot easily be reformed because too many vested interests have a stake in the existing system (Sampson, 2004). Nevertheless, British governments during the 1980s and since the late 1990s have presented themselves as engaged in a revolutionary programme of reform. A key element is a commitment to improving the efficiency of public services by introducing more competition and quality management techniques modelled on those used in manufacturing (Pollitt, 1993).

Clearly, much has changed during this period, and one can accept that in many respects the country is performing better economically by the measures used by governments to calculate international competitiveness.[3] Nevertheless, in many other respects, nothing has really changed, and one can argue that many public services have got worse. It takes longer to be admitted to hospital now than during the 1970s for many operations, even though there have been amazing advances in treatments. Rail services between major cities have become more unreliable, and certainly more expensive. There are fewer cheap local swimming pools or public libraries that contain a wide range of books. Many schools, outside the independent sector, are overcrowded, under-resourced and have high drop-out rates. A higher proportion of the population has the opportunity to experience higher education, but only through a significant drop in standards. Finally, crime continues to rise steadily, whichever political party holds power. One can, of course, debate these facts, but everyone knows that there is a significant gap between the apparent steady progress claimed by government ministers for their various areas of responsibility and our experience of these institutions in everyday life.[4]

So what then is the view of government in relation to achieving greater public accountability through audit and inspection? Writing as an insider based in the Financial Management Unit during the early 1980s, Spencer Zifcak (1994) chronicled the progress of a movement within the civil service promoting a greater emphasis on measurement and accountability in Britain. The literature suggests that there were unsuccessful earlier attempts by civil servants interested in new management methods to pursue this reform programme as early as the mid-1960s. The reform programme initiated by Margaret Thatcher's government was, by all accounts, only partially successful in the early 1980s. It was only in the late 1980s, and a testament to Thatcher's political will, that the Next Steps initiative achieved what some commentators describe as a 'revolution' in Whitehall.

By the 1990s, this drive to reform public institutions seemed to have run out of steam, unless one views John Major's 1992 Citizen's Charter (Cabinet Office, 1992) as a revolutionary initiative.[5] Nevertheless, the creation of Ofsted as a new inspectorate of education to replace what Conservative politicians saw as the failing system of Her Majesty's Inspectorates (Fitz-Gibbon and Stephenson-Forster, 1999) was highly significant, in that it set a standard for aggressive intervention into public institutions. Since 1997, the New Labour government has made improving the accountability of public services a central objective in its goal of modernising Britain.

One can use the public speeches of Tony Blair to identify some themes in this latest reform programme.

Economic change

As Prime Minister, Tony Blair has argued on a number of occasions that public service reform is required because otherwise Britain would fall behind in a rapidly changing world. Margaret Thatcher expressed similar sentiments during the 1980s when she argued that there was 'no alternative' to economic and governmental reform. To give an example, here is an extract from Tony Blair's speech to the Davos World Economic Forum on 18 January 2000:

> Technology and global financial markets are transforming our economy, our workplaces, our industrial structure. Economic change is uprooting communities and families from established patterns of life. The way we live, as well as the way we work, our culture, our shared morality, everything is under pressure from the intensity and pace of change. (PM's speeches, www.direct.gov.uk)

These and other speeches during his first term of office sound a little like the mid-19th-century *Communist manifesto*, authored by Karl Marx and Frederick Engels (1979), although the message is that there is no alternative to globalising capitalism, and the only solution for governments, as much as individuals or businesses, is to embrace ceaseless change. Interestingly, the base–superstructure model employed by Marx and Engels, which most social theorists today see as outdated and having little explanatory value, has a central place in these speeches. It is the global market economy and also sometimes new technology that is driving change, another theme in Marx's discredited writings.

The implications for business

The language used by Tony Blair in addressing the Confederation of British Industry, in a speech delivered on 11 November 1997, has a striking resemblance to the advice given to failing American companies in the late 1980s by the first management gurus. Indeed, he more or less committed the British government to the goal of 'continuous improvement':

> Today the Department of Trade and Industry (DTI) has published a report benchmarking the UK economy – comparing our performance with our competitors. It shows that while there are British firms competing effectively with the world's best, many are not. The message is clear: We need to redouble our efforts to match the standards set by the best companies in the world. And 'benchmarking' – seeking out and implementing Best Practice – can be a powerful tool for improving performance. (PM's speeches, www.direct.gov.uk)

W. Edwards Deming first suggested these remedies to improve the competitiveness of American manufacturing in the late 1970s. Two decades later, a British Prime Minister used a phrase invented by the quality movement when suggesting how to address similar problems in Britain. Whereas, however, Deming believed that governments, and bureaucratic regulation, should only have a limited role in managing the economy, Tony Blair in this speech was arguing that the British government still had an important role in improving performance. Instead of directly managing industry as happened during the 1960s, the state has become a management consultant, exhorting companies to employ techniques like benchmarking or fall behind international competition.

The rationale for public sector reform

The principal reason why New Labour won power in 1997 was because of growing disquiet, not only about economic management under the Conservatives following the disastrous attempt to join the European Exchange Rate Mechanism in 1992, but also about failing public services. To some extent, the same complaint has been heard at every significant election in Britain since the 1960s. It is generally recognised that there has been under-investment over many decades, and this was exacerbated by cuts and privatisation during the 1980s (Hutton, 1995). By the 1990s, this had become a central political issue. Governments had to demonstrate that they were most effective in fighting crime, raising educational standards, increasing university participation, reducing waiting lists in hospitals and making the trains run on time.[6]

In his first speech delivered to the civil service conference in 1997, Tony Blair praised civil servants for their expertise and dedication, and asked for their help in pursuing a reform programme designed to improve standards in delivering public services. The first step was the establishment of the Comprehensive Spending Review that gave departments more freedom in using budgets over a three-year period in return for meeting targets. In his 'Modernising public services' speech on 26 January 1999, Blair noted how this had implications for all levels of government:

> In turn, departments are setting standards for local public services to deliver – whether on exam results, rough sleepers, truancy or waiting lists. And local agencies are setting their own targets for local people to judge their success. (PM's speeches, www.direct.gov.uk)

The new government kept to tight spending limits in its first term of office. However, in the second term, there was an ambitious programme of investment, particularly in the National Health Service and education, launched in another series of speeches to the civil service conference. This spending programme was presented to the public as part of a programme of reform designed to improve efficiency and value for money in the public sector. The most controversial measures, announced in the public services speech delivered on 25 January 2001, were the introduction of teaching assistants in classrooms and more civilian staff in the police in order to reduce the cost of delivering services. There was also, however, even more emphasis on raising standards through inspection. In a speech on public sector reform, delivered on 16 October 2001, Blair explained how national standards would be used as benchmarks in health and education:

> In Health, there is now independent inspection of hospitals and the publication of results – the first national star ratings for each hospital in the country published two weeks ago and a National Institute of Clinical Excellence to set standards for best treatments across the NHS.

> In the police, we are driving up the performance of the weakest forces so that they match the performance of the best. David Blunkett is setting up a strong Police Standards Unit to spread Best Practice rapidly across the country. He will have powers of intervention where forces are failing. (PM's speeches, www.direct.gov.uk)

Although cynics and political opponents might see these speeches as simply a marketing exercise, designed to persuade a sceptical public that this government at least was serious about improving public services, one can see that real things were being done. A whole set of institutions and processes were established during the late 1990s to measure and raise standards. As Norman Fairclough (2000) has demonstrated, the whole language of government has changed, and positive phrases derived from quality management such as 'driving up' performance are used throughout the public sector.

Mechanisms of accountability

Although the current emphasis on measurement and inspection is a product of New Labour's political programme since the late 1990s, it also builds on a series of measures taken by the previous Conservative administrations, and seems likely to continue if there is a change in government. The whole system has grown gradually, and often outside political scrutiny, as a movement in government concerned with measuring and raising standards. This has included the development of performance indicators and league tables, the growth of auditing, a more interventionist role for inspectorates, and a greater requirement placed on publicly funded and voluntary agencies to evaluate their own activities. Although these developments have been discussed elsewhere (for example, Carter et al, 1992; Pollitt, 1993), a short summary will help to provide some context for understanding the work of inspectors, and how organisations have been affected by these changes.

Performance indicators

Remarkably, performance indicators, which many people working in the public sector take for granted, were only introduced into the British government during the early 1980s. Before then, it would appear that ministers only had a rough idea of what their departments were spending, the objectives of different agencies and whether these were achieved. This suggests that one can exaggerate the extent to which effective state bureaucracies, run on rational principles based on measuring achievements and costing programmes, had developed in industrialised countries during the late 19th and 20th centuries. It may only be in our own times that the processes described by Max Weber as rationalisation, at least in the area of government, are beginning to change publicly funded agencies and professional work.

Carter et al (1992) note that performance indicators were first introduced by the US Secretary of Defence Robert McNamara during the early 1960s, and this planning, programming and budgeting system was then extended by President Johnson to all areas of government. It ran into political problems, partly because there were not sufficiently developed 'informational resources and techniques' (Schick, 1969). In Britain, there were calls for introducing greater performance management in the 1968 Fulton Report:

> Accountable management means holding individuals and units responsible for performance measured as objectively as possible. Its achievement depends upon identifying or establishing accountable units within government departments – units where output can be measured as objectively as possible and where individuals can be held personally responsible for their performance. (Fulton, 1968, p 51)

This only started to happen systematically in the 1980s, through the Financial Management Initiative, and then the Next Steps programme of devolving responsibility to semi-autonomous agencies. The central mechanism that made the system possible was for every organisation to demonstrate performance using a set of indicators. These have evolved over time, and there have been many technical and political debates over the value of particular measures. Nevertheless, there is now a system in place in which every government agency, from the courts service to hospitals, has to provide performance information to government, as a condition of receiving public funding. In turn, government departments have to supply this information to the Treasury, and the amount they receive each year is partly determined by their success at meeting targets.

The remarkable success of these initiatives in changing the culture of organisations, and public attitudes, can be seen by considering two management tools that did not exist prior to 1980. The first is the league table, in which performance information is used by civil servants to encourage competition or enable stakeholders to raise questions locally. One can, for example, find information on government websites about the exam pass rate of different schools, or about the success rate for operations in different hospitals. The second is staff appraisal, the system in which employees at all levels are required to meet with a line manager once a year to set objectives. It is remarkable that, in the space of 20 years, organisations like the police or universities have moved from having no appraisal to establishing an elaborate system that both takes up a large amount of time for managers and other staff, and requires an expansion of human resources departments to maintain and update the records.

Auditing

Another important development during the 1980s was the growth of auditing. This began with the establishment of the Audit Commission in 1982 that conducts financial and performance reviews for local authorities. It was also charged with implementing an ambitious scheme in the 1990s to raise standards in local authorities by requiring them to set goals and review their own performance in the same way as businesses (Audit Commission, 1993). This was known as Best Value review, although it has since been relaunched as the Comprehensive Performance Assessment, partly because of complaints that inspections placed too great a burden on local agencies. These were required to conduct regular reviews of their own services, but in addition Best Value reviews were inspected by staff seconded to the Audit Commission from local government. These inspections did not simply examine documents, but involved conducting 'reality checks' through observing service delivery. The objective was to compare performance against national standards, so that inspectors compared the percentage of consumers satisfied with, for example, refuse collection against the national average in comparable authorities. They also sought to determine whether the service was likely to improve based on the authority's past record. This information was presented to local people and the authority as a 'simple matrix' so that they could 'easily assess the authority's performance, and how it compared with others' (Audit Commission, 1993, p 10).

Inspection

Although inspectorates have existed in Britain since the 19th century, they did not pursue a systematic programme of inspection, or make their findings available to the general public (Day and Klein, 1990). This has only happened relatively recently, since the 1990s, as the quality agenda has become institutionalised within the British public sector. It is significant that the inspectorates that have experienced most change are also those concerned with the most politically sensitive areas of policy. Ofsted was created during John Major's government not simply out of a desire to modernise, but also as a political measure to combat progressive ideas about education (Fitz-Gibbon and Stephenson-Forster, 1999). The objective behind the new national curriculum was to improve basic standards, and to impose central control over teachers who were seen as failing students. Her Majesty's Inspectors of Education, with their allies in the Department of Education and Science (DES), were seen as obstacles. Thomas (1999, p 136) supplies a revealing quote from the memoirs of Kenneth Baker, who was Secretary of State for Education towards the end of the 1980s:

> Of all Whitehall Departments, the DES was among those with the strongest in-house ideology. There was a clear 1960s ethos ... rooted in progressive orthodoxies.... It was devoutly anti-excellence, anti-selection and anti-market.... If civil servants were the guardians of this culture, then Her Majesty's Inspectors of Education were its priesthood. Reports on schools were written with an opaque quality which defied any reader to judge whether the school being inspected was any good or not. (Baker, 1993, p 168)

When Ofsted was set up by the 1992 Education (Schools) Act, it did not abolish Her Majesty's Inspectorates, but established a parallel, independent system. This was to inspect every school systematically on a five-year rolling programme, and provide information on 'strengths and weaknesses' to parents (DES, 1991). Since then, it has effectively taken over the previous system as a more interventionist agency that, while in some respects independent, actively promotes the government's programme of reforms.

The same argument can be made in relation to the other inspectorates created or reformed during the 1990s. The Quality Assurance Agency for Higher Education (QAA) was established in 1996, not simply to assure quality, but to encourage universities to adopt the reforms in the delivery of teaching and the curriculum required for the expansion of higher education. The establishment of a Commission for Health Improvement (CHI) in 2004 cannot be separated from reforms that have gradually introduced a market in health services over a 20-year period (Salter, 2004). The creation of the Police Standards Unit (PSU) in 2001 in the Home Office is one of the latest developments, and although it does not have the resources or remit of Ofsted, it is viewed by police forces as introducing a more interventionist form of inspection.[7]

Evaluation

As well as being accountable to government departments and audited and inspected by external bodies, public agencies also regularly evaluate their own activities. This has become part of good management practice, but it is also required under some legislative programmes. The 1997 Crime and Disorder Act, which created partnerships between state and voluntary agencies (an example of 'joined-up government'), requires that each partnership evaluate its activities.

In addition to having a regulatory role particularly over local government, the Audit Commission has conducted a series of evaluative reports about different aspects of the delivery of policy: what are sometimes called 'thematic inspections'. It also acts as a clearing-house for ideas about managing public sector organisations. Many of its reports offer management advice in the same way as consultants in the private sector (for example, Audit Commission, 1989).

More generally, the field of evaluation has been one of the fastest-growing areas in social science.[8] In America, it is dominated by quantitative researchers who conduct experimental studies through measuring inputs and outputs on randomised populations in government programmes, and trying to establish causal relationships. National funding bodies in the United Kingdom, such as the Economic and Social Research Council, and government agencies, such as the Home Office, have supported academic work of this kind, and indeed their mission statements encourage applicants to design projects that are sophisticated evaluation studies.

The largest growth area in evaluation research has, however, been small-scale studies conducted by consultants for local agencies, such as local councils, schools or voluntary organisations. Academic standards in these evaluations are usually low, given that they are intended to address the practical concerns of managers and local stakeholders, rather than be published in peer-reviewed journals.[9] They also inevitably often produce bland or comfortable findings that managers can use when applying for additional funding, or to demonstrate that they are satisfying a requirement to evaluate. Many of these consultants are based in universities, and evaluation studies have become an important source of research income. In this way, academics who in previous decades might have pursued scholarly or 'ivory tower' research are making their own contribution to the quality assurance industry.

The work of inspectorates

Most of the activities relating to quality assurance are of little interest to the general public. The Audit Commission has a local District Audit Office in most cities in the United Kingdom, but this is often discreetly located outside the city centre, and few people know about the services auditors perform for public bodies. It is certainly not perceived as a glamorous occupation. Television documentaries are routinely made about high-profile occupational groups such as lawyers, doctors and teachers who deal with the public, and scientists whose work can significantly affect our lives. Managers, accountants, lower-grade civil servants and quality assurers have not received the same attention, partly because the work of these occupations, and the people who perform it, are not considered entertaining or dramatic (Harper, 1989). The only recent exception is *The Office*, a television comedy that satirised modern rituals such as the performance appraisals and team-building exercises that take place in most businesses.

Another reason why not much has been written about these organisations is that it is hard for outsiders to obtain permission to observe the sensitive and private activities that take place behind the scenes. The following account looks at different aspects of the work of inspectorates, drawing on interviews and publicly available reports, including what is involved in making quality judgements, and the political nature of the task. To begin with, however, it is worth providing some details on the difficulties encountered in obtaining permission to study their work, which itself provides some interesting insights into this under-researched area of government.

Studying inspectorates

The author's first approach was to Ofsted, which is the largest inspectorate in the United Kingdom. It also has the highest public profile, given that the Chief Inspector between 1994 and 2000 was Chris Woodhead, an ex-teacher with an abrasive personality who conducted a campaign against underperforming schools, and against the teaching unions for resisting change. One entertaining public spectacle in Britain during this period was the annual conference of the National Union of Teachers, where the audience jeered and slow hand-clapped during Woodhead's speech. On one occasion, he was mobbed by protestors, and apparently had to hide in a cupboard while waiting to be rescued by his staff.

Woodhead had just resigned as Chief Inspector, partly owing to a politically motivated campaign about his private life, and was replaced by Mike Tomlinson, who immediately adopted a softer stance towards schools, and was viewed by some commentators as a safe pair of hands. Perhaps because senior managers were still worried about public criticism, Ofsted was unable to support the proposal, given that it wanted to look at political debates about quality assurance ('Quality assurance and its critics'). If the project had been framed as a neutral, technical study, then perhaps the outcome would have been different.[10]

Thinking that quality assurers concerned with the author's own occupation might support an ethnographic study, the next approach was to John Randall, then Chief Executive of the QAA. Randall is also a colourful and abrasive character, and his provocative views on falling standards were often reported by the media. During the late 1990s, he was trying to establish the second round of what was then called the Teaching Quality Assessment (TQA) in universities. However, he encountered stiff resistance from, among others, the Russell Group of universities that had good connections with politicians and the media, and were campaigning for a 'lighter touch' inspection for their own institutions.

Randall responded positively, but a month later he suddenly resigned as Chief Executive. Some commentators suggested that he had effectively been sacked by the DES for being too independent a regulator. When contacted, he said that he would still be happy to provide an interview. However, since he was now working as a consultant, he would need to charge £300 for an hour, considerably in excess of the sums that anthropologists normally pay informants. For those readers who are public service professionals on modest but steady incomes, this provides a glimpse into an unfamiliar social world.[11]

Most success in obtaining access to research data was achieved through approaching the five criminal justice inspectorates that deal with the police, the probation service, the Magistrates' Courts, the Crown Prosecution Service (CPS) and prisons. The Chief Inspector of Prisons, David Ramsbotham, was about to retire after having become a thorn in the side of the government during his period of office through publishing many hard-hitting reports, and publicising his dissatisfaction with senior managers in the prisons service and government ministers through the press (Ramsbotham, 2005). He was also enthusiastic about the idea that independent academic research should be conducted about inspections.

His successor, Anne Owers, was less interested, partly because she was new to a sensitive post.[12] All the criminal justice inspectorates, however, were under pressure to do more without new resources, and it was hard arranging appointments with senior managers. In addition, they were being reviewed by two separate government inquiries, which one informant felt might result in them being merged into a super-inspectorate, which would inevitably result in job losses.[13] This was one polite reason given why managers could not spend a great deal of time assisting a researcher, aside from allowing a few interviews. Staff and management time was already tied up in preparing for these internal inspections.

Two additional experiences are worth reporting that convey a sense of how these organisations deal with outsiders. Rod Morgan was then Her Majesty's Chief Inspector of Probation, a criminologist who had moved into government after a career in policy research.[14] A thoughtful and politically astute civil servant, he immediately suggested that the problem for researchers lay in the fact that government really was a different world. Rather than looking at his own inspectorate, he suggested a focus on the inspectorate responsible for overseeing the CPS. This made sense because the author could draw on his own legal background (having qualified as a solicitor before becoming a sociologist), and previous experience of studying legal practice. At the same time, an approach could be made to a management committee for the five inspectorates, which he chaired.

Her Majesty's Crown Prosecution Service Inspectorate agreed to consider the request, provided that permission was first obtained from the management committee. The management committee for the five inspectorates said it could review the request, but only when the backing of a particular inspectorate had been secured. Those who enjoyed the classic British comedy series *Yes, Minister* may be pleased to know that delaying tactics of this kind, or what some might view as bureaucratic inertia, are alive and well in Whitehall. A second experience illustrates how difficult it is, in practice, to research sensitive organisations. Through the good offices of Her Majesty's Inspectorate of Probation, contact was made with the Crown Prosecution Service Inspectorate. The organisation it inspects still has a reputation, certainly among the legal profession, for being under-resourced and badly managed. There have also been a number of public scandals about what professionals call 'cracked trials': cases where the judge stops the trial on the grounds that there is flawed or insufficient evidence, after literally millions have been spent preparing the case. In contrast to the prison service or the police, no academic studies have been conducted in Britain about the CPS, or at least none based on long periods of observation or access to staff. The inspectorate was interested in supporting a study based on observing inspections, but only if it obtained permission from senior managers in the CPS. They politely declined to participate.

Methodologies of inspection

The idea of using scientific methods to improve the efficient working of society can be traced back to French writers like Condorcet, Saint-Simon, Comte and the statistician Quetelet during the 18th and early 19th centuries. To some extent, these early social scientists were intellectualising what was happening inside the new manufacturing industries that rapidly developed during this period as engineers and entrepreneurs worked out how to improve the productivity of machinery and labour. The academic route led to the sophisticated methods used to make causal findings such as randomised trials that are now widely employed and, in some cases, even required in government research programmes.[15] The practical work of managers (Clegg, 1990) and quality assurers involves rough and ready tools of observation and counting, and interpreting different measures of performance. What they have in common is a belief that one can collect data that objectively describe or represent what happens inside organisations, through using scientific procedures like sampling. There are some quantitative researchers in universities who would see these methods as insufficiently thoughtful or scientific (for example, Pawson and Tilley, 1997); and others might question whether objectivity can so easily be obtained on philosophical grounds. Quality assurers are not, however, troubled by these concerns; or at least they are irrelevant or inappropriate to the practical task at hand.[16]

A flavour of the practical and matter-of-fact, but also methodical, character of inspection can be found in the following details supplied by staff working for three criminal justice inspectorates about the process of inspection. They have some similarities, but also show how methodologies have developed differently, according to the problems faced by each inspectorate.

Her Majesty's Magistrates' Courts Service Inspectorate

This was established in 1993, and was responsible for inspecting the 42 Magistrates' Court Committees in the United Kingdom. It is based in modern, open-plan offices on a government site, originally an army barracks, on the outskirts of Bristol. As in the case of the other inspectorates, at the time of the author's visit a few people were at their workstations writing up reports. Most were, however, away conducting on-site inspections.

When it was first established, the work of an inspector involved spending several months a year visiting courts around the country. However, the recent senior management team had devised a more efficient way of meeting its objectives. The new system involved developing a judgement on the basis of analysing documentary records, and visiting for short periods with more focused questions. It was also now possible to exercise discretion so that an institution could receive a lighter inspection, which would happen if it had received good reports in previous rounds. These changes have also taken place independently in other inspectorates. This may be because they share ideas through informal channels of communication, but the most likely explanation is that all agencies that inspect a large number of organisations, with limited resources, face the same problems over time, and will develop similar solutions.

Inspections were carried out by three people, a lead inspector and two others, who met and took key decisions in consultation with a senior manager. The methodology had developed over time and was available in two guides, as the interviewee explained:

> 'There is a handbook for inspectors which explains broadly
> how we do what we are doing. This breaks the inspection
> down into a number of stages and includes an internal
> timetable saying what has to be done within what timescales,
> and who is responsible for carrying it out. Then there is an
> inspection manual, which is a technical document that sets
> out some of the legal framework within which MCCs
> [Magistrates' Court Committees] have to operate. That's
> really a reference for inspectors so if they have a query or
> are uncertain about something they can go back and get a
> simple explanation in the handbook, and usually a reference
> to primary legislation.'

The process started with a letter from the Chief Inspector sent to the chair of an MCC, giving details of the inspection team and the 'key functions' they would be investigating. These were currently strategic management, corporate governance, human resources and the administration of cases:

> 'The first step with the letter is to ask them to conduct a
> self-assessment process: what they think their key strengths

and weaknesses are ... to provide evidence and commentary on these. They also have to let us know their main areas of activity, and what they are still planning to do.'

The inspectorate also wrote asking for 'briefing material'. This included documentary information such as strategic plans, annual reports, performance monitoring reports, minutes of committee meetings, senior management meetings and copies of various policies and procedures. This often arrived neatly packaged in bankers' boxes that could contain a few thousand sheets of paper. The shelves along one wall of this inspector's office were filled with 12 boxes: the briefing material that had arrived for an inspection of a large Magistrates' Court area.

While waiting for the documentation, the inspection team also 'conducted a questionnaire exercise', which involved sending a questionnaire to court users. These included all the magistrates working in the courts, and representatives from the other criminal justice agencies such as the police, the CPS, the probation service, Youth Offending Teams, the local authorities and local solicitors firms. The questionnaires:

> 'invite them ... to score the MCC on a number of issues, such as the quality of information they had received, how much they had been informed about the strategic plans of the MCC and how much they were able to influence that ... and they also have the opportunity to put some textual comments giving their own view.'

The first stage of the inspection was based on the analysis of the self-assessment report, the briefing papers, the questionnaire responses, and also 'hard data analysis' of the statistical performance data, the information the local management teams supplied to the Lord Chancellor's Department (as it then was) as performance indicators on listing times. It also, however, involved a short visit to the Magistrates' Court area. The inspection team conducted observation in courthouses and interviewed representatives from the police, CPS, probation service and local authority, following up issues raised in the questionnaires.

After collecting this information, the team was then in a position to develop an initial 'hypothesis'. The interviewee's account of how this happened gives a sense both of the serious and methodical character of the inspection process, and the amount of work involved in reaching a preliminary collective judgement:

A: Having gone through everything, each inspector produces a written hypothesis paper which assesses the MCC against each defining element of the key functions as laid down in the inspection framework.

Q: How long are these documents?

A: They would be anything from 10 pages up to 30 or 40 pages, obviously depending on the size of the organisation being assessed and the amount of evidence. The papers are a hypothesis of how well the MCC is meeting defining elements of the key function, and then the evidence to support that in the central column, and then another column which is what further evidence is needed, what questions we are going to ask and what documentation we need to see to satisfy ourselves if we are not clear on a particular issue. So, they act both as a hypothesis we are going to test, and as a way of recording what other information we need to test that hypothesis.

Q: And is there a meeting?

A: We have a formal hypothesis meeting, which for an amalgamated MCC lasts two days.

Q: Two days?

A: Oh yes. It is vitally important that each of us is clear on all of the key functions. Although we are leading on one or two, we will in the course of the main fieldwork period be interviewing a number of staff across a range of key functions, so we need a clear understanding of the issues.

Having modified and agreed on the hypotheses, the next stage is to meet with senior managers and test them. An example would be that the documents had suggested there was a problem with the way the MCC was using its financial resources:

'We would sit down in one to one interviews and say that in our view this MCC is not using its resources effectively. "This is because your budgets do not show that you are spending in accordance with your strategic plan, and we don't believe that the percentage of money you spend on secretariat staff as opposed to operational staff is appropriate. How do you feel about that?" This gives them an opportunity to reply, and to clarify the statistics.'

After this visit, described as the 'main fieldwork stage', the team held a second 'judgement meeting'. This reviewed the evidence against the hypotheses, and identified strengths and weaknesses in the MCC being inspected. The aim was to arrive at specific evaluative judgements and recommendations. To give an example, on a recent inspection the team had asked the management team to develop a human resources strategy, which this area did not have since it was still struggling with issues relating to the amalgamation. It was also asked to monitor the effectiveness of the strategy; in other words, to demonstrate results at the next inspection in two years' time.

Her Majesty's Inspectorate of Constabulary

The methodology here had also changed. Whereas this inspectorate once conducted inspections of forces, now it inspected Basic Command Units (BCUs) on a three-year cycle. This was a major increase in workload, and yet there had been no increases in staffing. There were two inspectors in each team, and they assessed the three areas of 'operations and performance', 'corporate governance' and 'community engagement'. A similar, if less drawn-out and elaborate, procedure was involved:

> 'There is some work and analysis prior to the inspection – of performance data [which is compared to the Chief Constable's self-assessment]. They visit the BCU for a few hours and meet the management team. They explain the process and agree a timetable. They then go back for four days…. This is normally Tuesday to Friday, and on Friday they meet with the BCU commander and his or her management team.'

Her Majesty's Crown Prosecution Service Inspectorate

This inspectorate had developed a system that reduced the level of inspections for areas considered to be low risk. Again, this was established on methodical grounds:

'As part of our new methodology, we do risk assessment on areas in order to decide, first of all, if it is going to be a full inspection or an intermediate inspection. And in order to do that we look at the data, which is held centrally, which would include things like performance on persistent young offenders, cracked and ineffective trials, things like that. We would also look at the last report to see what the position was then.'

This part of the interview also provides a glimpse of the work involved in implementing a new system:

Q: Is it easy to know whether it should be a full inspection?

A: It is not that easy – bear in mind, it is only the first batch that we have done. I personally have only been involved in risk assessing two. We were doing it by two inspectors coming up with an assessment. You score it. You look at the various criteria and you give it a score, and your overall score will determine where the area falls within a number of areas.

This inspectorate differed from the other criminal justice inspectorates visited in that it did not confine itself to assessing the performance of management. A business management inspector looked at the performance of management and corporate governance issues. This side of the inspection had been introduced relatively recently following a programme of reform initiated by the 1998 Glidewell Report. There was also a legal inspector who looked at the quality of decision making. In this respect, the CPS inspectorate had more in common with inspectorates that are concerned with health and education: these do not simply look at whether schools and hospitals are well managed, but at the delivery of services. This provides more scope for potential tension with professionals, who might feel that outsiders are unqualified to assess their work on the basis of an inspection visit or documentary analysis.

In the case of the CPS, the possibility of disagreement was reduced through restricting the scope of the legal inspector to the test used in the High Court to determine whether a decision was the kind that 'no reasonable prosecutor could make'. To make this assessment, two legal inspectors went through a sample of files using a checklist. An extract from the interview gives an indication of the amount of work involved:

'On the casework side, we get numerous files, hundreds of files. I cannot remember exactly, but in this case it was about 300. They are asked to pick particular files in case categories. They come in boxes, but in addition you have the management information which comes in different ways, depending on the area. There is a checklist of all the management information we require, and some areas will put that all in order, numbered in several ring-binders.'

The inspectors went through the files with a questionnaire, using a handbook 'that has guidance on how to interpret and answer each of the questions'. It took about four weeks looking through these, and the documents relating to management, 'to work out what the issues were'.

Making quality judgements

In constructionist studies about the work of scientists, judges and teachers, the fact that professionals exercise judgement is sometimes presented as a means of undermining the objectivity of the facts obtained through employing these investigative methods (see, for example, Latour and Woolgar, 1986). The fact that the findings that appear in scientific journals result from argument and interpretation in laboratories, and that journal articles themselves are interpreted in assessing the significance and validity of findings, has been used to undermine philosophical claims about the inevitability of scientific progress. A key issue raised by researchers in the sociology of scientific knowledge is that decisions are often made on extra-scientific or political grounds. In simple terms, the status of someone speaking in a meeting, and their powers of persuasion, may be more important than the strength of a case in winning an argument.

One interesting feature of fact-finding organisations is that a mechanism always exists to close off legitimate disagreement beyond a certain point, subject perhaps to an appeals procedure that can be accessed at some time in the future through legitimate channels. In courts of law dealing with criminal offences, it is accepted that magistrates and jurors will disagree in interpreting facts, and judges at all levels will disagree over applying the law. In some types of case, where there is no evidence other the claims made by witnesses, reaching a decision can be extremely difficult. An example is the work of adjudicators deciding appeals by asylum-seekers applying to stay in the United Kingdom (Travers, 1999). Assuming the appellant came from a country where it was agreed that political persecution was taking place (which itself could be subject to dispute), it was not at all easy to tell whether someone had been tortured or was making up a story. During the late 1990s, there was a high refusal rate for many of these countries, despite the fact that appellants had to satisfy a low burden of proof. Critics suggested that this demonstrated there was a 'culture of refusal' among adjudicators, or that over time they became case-hardened through dealing with so many appeals that had clearly been fabricated.

Another example is the judgements made in marking essays or examinations at university level. We know that markers develop short cuts over time, so that rather than having to read every word of a script, they can obtain enough information to make an assessment by reading part of an essay or skimming through paragraphs in a kind of sampling procedure. Research studies have also shown that standards and marking criteria can differ considerably between institutions and individuals. The elaborate second-marking procedures employed in some institutions to ensure an objective standard often result in wide differences between marks, which are resolved either through the decision of a third marker or external examiner, or by amicably agreeing to split the difference. Finally, although most marking systems, outside formative assessments, involve anonymised marking, in practice teachers often know something about the motivation and ability of their students. One can make too crude a distinction between how professionals distinguish between 'worthy' and 'unworthy' clients (see Lipsky, 1980): but marking, like any form of decision making, involves judgement and discretion, as opposed to the mechanical application of rules.

In the case of inspections, it is difficult obtaining access to the meetings where decisions are made. It is, however, possible to make some general comparative points. First, it is clear that making judgements about quality requires the exercise of discretion, and that decision makers can disagree. This can happen at the stage of determining whether a light or full inspection is appropriate. It is also relevant to judgement meetings:

Q: Are individual views expressed in the meeting that result in changes to the hypotheses?

A: Absolutely. That's the whole purpose of the meeting. The inspector leading on a particular function speaks to the written hypothesis on each key function, and summarises the evidence that supports that, and then the rest of the team, and indeed the director who is there in a Quality Assurance role, ask questions if they are not clear, seek clarifications, suggest modifications to the wording or provide contrary evidence which they may have found from another source but has not been taken into account. So it is an extremely iterative process. The initial hypothesis which comes to the meeting rarely survives without modification, and in some cases is severely modified.

Another example is the process of checking files by the CPS inspectorate to check whether they met the reasonableness test used by the High Court. In this case, procedures had been developed to produce consistency across different inspections:

> 'You have the framework document and you have very detailed guidance on the questions. There is an issue on consistency but that tends to be whether, if you answer 'Yes' to one question, the following question should be a 'Yes' or a 'Not applicable' or a 'Not known'. This is something we do need to address and we have just done an exercise in consistency following the first six reports to check the data to see if we were being consistent. In relation to decision making, if any of us is not sure how to answer a question, they will discuss it with someone else.'

How interviewees report this 'iterative', evidence-based process will inevitably conceal the methods used in these meetings to make findings of fact. The ethnomethodologist Harold Garfinkel (1984) documented these methods using examples of how coders deal with medical files. They include the documentary method of interpretation where one builds up a picture over time, but can revise the 'underlying pattern' as new evidence is discovered. Another is the procedure known as 'let it pass', where some piece of discrepant evidence is ignored because it might cause complications for a developing theory. There is also the interesting, but under-studied, phenomenon of how local precedents are created by a group of decision makers, and then modified in the light of difficult circumstances. This kind of analysis is not, however, meant to question the conclusions reached, but to allow us to appreciate the work involved in any kind of decision making.

The inspection visit

The on-site visit by a team of inspectors is the most visible feature of auditing and inspection. As Richard Harper (2000) has argued, irrespective of what the inspectors actually do there are some powerful symbolic messages being conveyed: that the organisation is under scrutiny, and the public sector is open and accountable. Since it was not possible to attend an inspection visit, this study cannot describe in any detail how a team forms a judgement through interviewing people, visiting work sites, or observing work, and the extent to which this modifies a judgement made on the basis of paper documents. However, it is possible to learn something about the process from interviews. One inspector said that getting the 'smell of a corridor' does make a difference. This suggests that the impressions one obtains through face-to-face contact can, in intangible ways, affect a judgement.

If taken literally, or even half literally, this raises some interesting issues. How is the corridor of a well-run custodial institution, for example, meant to smell?[17] Is it possible to reach a judgement about morale in an institution from looking at noticeboards, or the way people greet each other in corridors? We make these judgements all the time when visiting institutions as customers or clients, and know that they are, to some extent, seeking to manage our impressions. An example might be whether, all other things being equal, the way someone is dressed can influence a decision on objective criteria in a job interview. It is hard to know the extent to which these necessarily subjective judgements matter in inspections. As one might expect, this issue is not discussed in inspection reports.

Speaking to inspectors, one gets the sense that drawing conclusions from observation does not present any real interpretive problems. Here, for example, are some reflections on what you can see by sitting in a courtroom:

> 'There are some things you cannot get a flavour of just from the documentation like listing policy until you actually go and sit in a courthouse and see how the business flows on the day, and see how long a day lasts, and how long defendants are waiting in the waiting areas, and how long defendants in custody have to wait before they are seen by the duty solicitor, or taken up into court, and those kind of issues. You can only get that from physically sitting there all day observing and making notes.'

This inspector acknowledged that impression management took place, but felt that it was difficult to hide a sudden change of procedures:

> 'It's usually a dead give-away because if they start to run their court in a way which is not normal for that area, the other people in the court are usually extremely surprised. Most people don't bother.'

There was also no naive reliance on quantitative indicators, even though these are given most emphasis in reports. The role of this inspector was similar to that of an ethnographer trying to understand a different culture:

> 'Each court is a virtually stand-alone unit in terms of performance on the day. There will be a fairly standard listing procedures and similar practices across all of the courts, but a lot of what happens can be determined by the

Figure 4.1: Spending on inspection and external review, 1998/99 to 2003/04

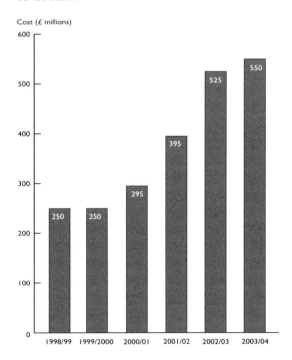

Cost (£ millions)

Source: HM Treasury. Originally published in *Inspecting for Improvement* (Office of Public Services Reform, 2003)

physical geography of the building, the culture within the area, the personalities of the CPS and defence solicitors. Any number of factors can impact on the way the court runs. And those are never discernible except by actually sitting there.'

Finally, there was also no naivety about what one can learn from conducting a few visits:

'We are aware that it is just a snapshot. But by going to a number of different courthouses, and seeing a number of different cases, we hope to get a reasonable picture of what the organisation is like. We would never make any judgements on the basis of a single piece of evidence collected at a single site, we just don't work like that. But it gives us the flavour of the organisation as a whole.'

During the TQA visits that took place in British universities in the mid-1990s, inspectors were given checklists to note whether students seemed engaged by a lecturer or if they were using an overhead projector (seen as a progressive teaching method as against delivering a lecture without visual aids). This answer, however, suggests that at least some inspectors see their task in broader terms: to understand the culture of an organisation, albeit on the basis of a few short visits.

The politics of inspection

There is a political element to all forms of assessment whenever factors external to the normal exercise of professional judgement become relevant or affect how decisions are made. An example from higher education is that lecturers are often reluctant, when marking a set of scripts, to find too many fails. This is not because the lecturer wants to avoid possible unpleasantness, or perhaps an appeal, from a failed student who has little influence as a consumer or customer. The political consideration is rather that the institution itself may have a policy, formal or otherwise, that too many fails are undesirable, especially if it is assessed on this performance indicator.

One interesting feature of inspections is that the managerial teams being inspected normally have a number of opportunities to influence the inspection. To give an example, the CPS inspectorate held a meeting shortly after the site visit when the preliminary findings were presented to the management team:

'It gives them the opportunity of querying anything they don't agree with or comes as a surprise to them. So at that meeting, it gives the opportunity for both the area and us to discuss any areas where there are conflicts. This gives us an opportunity to inform the area and see if they will agree with our findings, but also give us the opportunity to gain information that we may not have been given when we went on site.... The aim is to make sure any issues are resolved before the draft report is presented to them.'

This is another case where an interview cannot address what actually happens in these meetings, and how participants interpret them as political actions. It would appear that, in the majority of cases, there is very little disagreement, and this is confined to concerns (as opposed to complaints) about single words or phrases used in particular sections of reports. An NHS quality manager who had experience of inspecting hospitals did, however, provide an interesting insight into the politics of health inspections:

A: I remember we were at a hospital in London, and we were interviewing a porter, and he came out with something, and I thought, 'That just ain't right', you know. If we came across anything like that, that was so dodgy, it had to be brought to the attention of the CHI review manager immediately.

Q: Did it get into the final report?

A: I'm not sure if it got into the final report. Because that was the interesting thing, there was the stuff that gets in the final report and there is the other stuff. There was another one that I went to in, well I won't say where it was, a big, big teaching hospital, a very ambitious Chief Executive, had the ear of [...], and the CHI review manager copied in all the e-mails to us as a team going between her and the Chief Executive. And this Chief Executive was effectively bullying the CHI reviewer to get the report that he wanted because it had an impact on the star ratings. So he was debating the scores.... And the team I was in was a very experienced team, a very good CHI reviewer, an experienced consultant on the team, a very powerful team. There was a guy on the team called [...], very powerful, and it was just fascinating the politics that were going on.

Q: Did they get their way in the end?

A: They got their way a lot, yeah.

What is interesting about these inspections, at least as reported by this informant, is that there is often a status differential between members of the reviewing team (he was an ex-nurse) and the senior management teams in hospitals. To do the job of inspection properly required political backing from the Department of Health, but also people with weight and experience on the inspection team. It is also worth noting that it is only in some areas of public services that the grading from an inspection is used in allocating resources. This is not meant to suggest that inspections, or for that matter performance generally, is not taken seriously by management teams. One can see, however, that the reason this Chief Executive officer tried to influence the decision was because his hospital was hoping to achieve a star grading. The fact that few important consequences flow from the average inspection may explain why there is no right of appeal.

The goal of continuous improvement

Inspection forms one element in the broader activities summarised at the start of this chapter, which are informed by the goal of achieving 'continuous improvement' in the delivery of public services. Many people working in this field are, themselves, reflective about how quality can be measured and improved, so it is worth identifying some problems that inspectors and quality managers will readily acknowledge about the process of inspection and reliance on performance indicators. The chapter concludes with some thoughts on the interpretive and practical work required to maintain this system of regulation.

Problems with audit and inspection

Audit and inspection are each based on the assumption that the performance of organisations can be measured, and more generally that improvement can be demonstrated over time. Because of this, there tends to be an emphasis on quantifiable, performance indicators as against subjective measures. It is assumed that one can produce league tables that rank institutions such as schools and hospitals using objective criteria, and supply these with meaningful targets.

There are many problems associated with performance indicators, but it is worth mentioning two that are recognised by everyone in the public sector. The first is that a political directive to satisfy certain performance indicators may lead to performance in other areas being neglected. This can happen in higher education where students find they focus on assessments, as against growing intellectually through wide reading and discussion (Becker et al, 1961). The same problem faces managers in police forces or hospitals faced with regular inspections, or where they are required to report achievements in key areas.

The second is that one cannot be certain in any national exercise that one is comparing like with like. Part of the massive work expended on ensuring that objective comparisons can be made about police statistics will be described in the next chapter. It is common knowledge, however, that the ranking order in league tables is not usually determined by factors within the control of management. Studies have, for example, shown that league tables on exam performance in schools in England and Wales are uncannily similar to the rankings one can obtain using socioeconomic data about their pupils (Mulberg, 2000). This means that publishing league tables of every school, as if it means something, or tells us anything about teaching or management, is potentially misleading. The difficulty then arises that members of the general public or journalists cannot understand tables or diagrams that rank organisations using more sophisticated criteria.

Inspectorates have their own problems, and one of these stems from the fact that there are not sufficient resources to allow them to inspect organisations across the whole of the United Kingdom on a regular basis. This is not a trivial problem in that an inspection every six years, while generating a lot of concern in an institution, and possibly having important financial consequences, clearly allows a lot to happen in the period between inspections. At worst, one can imagine that it has a distorting effect, as great effort is made prior to the inspection, before the organisation returns to business as usual.[18]

Another set of problems that inspectorates face results from the conflicting demands of producing evaluative reports and helping institutions to improve. To give an example, the Magistrates' Court inspectorate spreads best practice informally through inspections because institutions are open about their problems. It even assigns 'liaison officers' to courts between assessment to assist with implementing the recommendations, and to provide general support. Because of this the inspectorate could be accused of having too close a relationship with the organisations it inspects. This has, however, only been seen as a problem since the 1990s when politicians started to realise that there were electoral gains from taking a tough stance on 'failing' institutions.[19]

Making the system work

These problems are not viewed as severe inside inspectorates or the quality assurance industry more generally, although they have led some critics to conclude that too much money is spent on auditing and inspection in Britain, or even that the whole exercise is a meaningless ritual (see the discussion of this critical literature in Chapter Seven). Ultimately, the system works because everyone, including members of the public, politicians, managers and inspectors, believes that the reports and figures produced are objective measures of performance. Against this, however, it is clear that a great deal of interpretive work is involved at all levels. Performance indicators can hardly be objective measures if resources are shifted between priorities within institutions to satisfy the current requirement from government. If inspectors disagree, and the organisation being inspected also disagrees, with an assessment, even if it does not have the political clout to influence the report, then one cannot talk of objectivity in a strong sense.

Against this, one might argue that the objectivity in these reports is the strongest we have, and this is why they are taken seriously. A flavour of the practical, matter-of-fact character of inspection can be found in the following answer given by a constabulary inspector. She was asked if it was easy to find evidence that demonstrated whether there was adequate management and leadership in a police force. This is, after all, something on which employees or fellow managers might disagree, and cannot be measured in the same way as manufactured products can be measured to meet a quality standard. From her perspective, however, it was relatively easy to make an objective judgement:

> 'There is usually some evidence. If someone has been in charge of a BCU for three years and performance has stagnated or deteriorated, the issue is that he or she has not got a grip on things. Another case might be that performance could be OK, but levels of sickness are up. We always talk to the Staff Association and the Police Federation, and they will tell us. And we also see the staff in focus groups. We see 60 people in the BCU, and they don't know in advance whom we want to see. We do reality checks – for example, we might arrive in the custody room unannounced. And if there is a staff suggestion scheme on the internet or the intranet, we can see their views on the shift system. Then we can look at staff bulletins and briefings, and the quality of this information, and how people find

out about things. Is it on the grapevine or is there a proper structure for communication? And we look at sickness notes. And we do triangulations, and we look for problems in other ways.'

At the root of audit and inspection is a belief that one can make factual judgements by assessing evidence. There is a matter-of-fact character to the way quality assurers present their activities that should disturb any postmodern sceptic, and underpins the rationalist assumption that every organisation can improve.

Notes

[1] For some practical guides, see Ellis (1988), Skelcher (1992), Gaster and Squires (1993) and Gaster (1995).

[2] Some researchers and government agencies might argue that the only way of producing useful or objective findings is to conduct a large number of interviews within an evaluative framework (see, for example, Davies et al, 2000; Wiles, 2002). From an interpretive perspective in sociology, the problem is that the local context or meaningful character of the activities they are describing disappears when the data are analysed.

[3] One example is that the proportion of the population entering higher education in the United Kingdom has increased to approaching 50 per cent owing to a policy decision to expand universities (Dearing, 1997).

[4] For a political argument along these lines directed against the Conservative Party, at a time when Labour seemed unelectable, see Hutton (1995). The same criticisms could be made of New Labour's achievements in office: that nothing has substantially changed.

[5] In retrospect, the Citizen's Charter was an important initiative that set targets and promised league tables for the first time in Britain. It is today mostly remembered for establishing the 'cones hotline' in June 1992 that allowed concerned citizens to report unattended cones on motorways.

[6] The political challenge faced by British governments in recent times has been in trying to improve public services while maintaining the support of well-off voters who would prefer lower levels of taxation,

privatised services and privileged access to higher education. For a perceptive analysis of class politics in Britain, see Parkin (1972).

[7] The PSU has already intervened in 'failing' police forces, and resulted in the replacement of some Chief Police Officers. Some interviewees for this study suggested that Her Majesty's Inspectorate of Constabulary had too close a relationship with the police. It had lost the confidence of ministers and might eventually be replaced by the PSU.

[8] For an introduction, see Weiss (1998).

[9] For discussion, see Travers (2005a and 2005b).

[10] This rather nicely encapsulates the relationship between sociologists and many official institutions at the present time. As in the 1950s, it is wise to play down any political debates relevant to a topic, and instead present yourself as a technical expert interested in serving the needs of government. This also explains the popularity of 'evidence-based' research in Britain and America. In looking for 'what works', based on measuring quantitative indicators, supported by interviews in a narrowly evaluative framework, one is usually precluded from considering the views of critics, not least in this case the teachers affected by Ofsted inspections.

[11] Randall was later appointed as Chief Executive of another regulatory agency. He is one of a pool of experienced and qualified senior managers who can take on these leadership positions. As in the private sector, there are inevitable risks when taking on a high-profile appointment, although, no doubt, there are generous severance packages.

[12] An insider later revealed that she had behaved extremely skilfully during this period in increasing the resources available to the inspectorate against opposition from ministers.

[13] This looks likely to happen (Office of Public Services Reform, 2003), although it remains to be seen whether there will be significant job losses through creating a super-inspectorate. It is, for example, possible that this could create an extra tier of administration.

[14] He subsequently became head of the Youth Justice Board.

[15] The 2001 No Child Left Behind Act makes randomised trials, described as 'evidence-based' research, mandatory for anyone doing funded research on schools in the USA.

[16] There are some sociologists or cultural commentators who might want to challenge the objectivity of quality reports by showing that they are 'constructed'. From this perspective, each and every fact in a report represents an interpretive judgement. The deconstructionist philosopher Jacques Derrida (1978) took this a step further and argued that all facts are indeterminate, subject to endless interpretation. From another perspective, factual findings about the world are made, every day, without any great difficulty, even about matters that require judgement and interpretation, such as whether someone has accomplished a work task effectively. These may sometimes be challenged or contested, but by ordinary members of society, and not on philosophical grounds. The task for an ethnomethodological researcher is to describe how this gets done; or, to put it in grander terms, to describe how society works in a way that preserves how we experience and understand society as an objective reality in everyday life. See Schutz (1973); and, for discussion of constructionism, Travers (2004).

[17] The real issue here is, probably, when does a bad smell become an accountable matter? Is it ordinary or unusual, given what one expects to find in such settings, and, if the latter, how is this explained by those responsible for the corridor? On the different ways in which the run-down reception of a business can be explained, see Travers (1997, ch 2).

[18] A good example is the Research Assessment Exercise in British universities. Once details of the test were published, and as new details emerged, institutions devised and implemented strategies. This could involve investing resources in 'research-active' staff or buying in new talent, sometimes just for the period of the exercise.

[19] One could argue that this new approach to inspection actually produces failure.

FIVE

Organisations and accountability

The growth of public sector management
Quality assurance in universities
—   Assessment
—   Feedback forms
—   Annual monitoring
—   Accreditation
—   External inspections
Quality assurance in a police force
—   Internal inspection
—   Best Value inspection
—   Baseline inspection
—   Crime recording
The costs of quality
—   Managing professionals
—   The demands of auditing and inspection

The previous chapter reviewed some of the measures and initiatives taken by British governments since the 1980s to improve the effectiveness and accountability of public sector organisations, focusing on the work of inspectorates. A great deal of time is now spent in institutions such as schools, hospitals, universities, the police, local government, and many agencies in the voluntary sector in preparing for inspections by different central agencies. However, although this is the most dramatic side of quality assurance, it does not fully convey the extent of the cultural shift that has taken place in organisations, the procedures and practices involved or the overlap between different forms of regulation and self-assessment. This chapter describes in more detail the quality assurance procedures and systems employed in three institutions, a 'new' and 'old' university and a police force. It will also make some observations on the different perspectives of managers and professionals towards professional work. To begin with, however, it considers the growth of management as an occupation in recent times.

The growth of public sector management

Management has been the fastest-growing occupation in mature industrial societies for the last century (Mintzberg, 1973; Salaman, 1995). Public and private sector organisations have grown massively during this period, as the number of workers required to produce goods and services has been reduced, so ever more managers and administrators are required to process information and organise the production process.[1] Frederick Taylor (1990), the founder of scientific management, argued in the 1930s that it would be cost-effective to employ three technical experts for each labourer in a brick yard: this would increase both output and quality through ensuring that the materials were in the right place at the right time, and workers' bodies were used effectively.

Although it would be hard to find an organisation where managers and administrative staff outnumber workers to this degree, management has grown in the way Taylor predicted. Many of the new positions created are concerned with systematic record keeping, which only became possible as a result of technical and organisational advances during the 1940s and 1950s (Wheeler, 1976). The modern hospital and university produce and store vast amounts of information on individuals as part of their routine operations. Moreover, all organisations now document and monitor the performance of employees for internal purposes in many ways. Human resources departments, for example, barely existed in organisations during the 1970s, whereas today they employ large numbers of specialist professionals.

At the risk of oversimplifying, management jobs can be divided into three categories. Senior managers, such as the chief executives of hospitals and vice-chancellors in universities, have often risen from the ranks within organisations, although there is an increasing tendency to bring in expertise from outside. This layer of public administration has also become, to some extent, professionalised, with managers holding permanent positions, attending courses in management theory and learning to talk in a specialist language. They are often physically separated from the rest of the staff (for example, in an administrative floor at the top of a hospital). They also dress differently and are sometimes described disparagingly as 'suits' in schools and hospitals. Middle managers, by contrast, usually continue to work in professional roles, but are responsible for ensuring that directives or policies devised by senior management are followed by those delivering services. They, therefore, have divided loyalties and can experience role conflict. In organisations undergoing organisational change, they are often required to explain unpopular changes (for example, increases in workload) to the staff they manage. However, they do not necessarily have a harmonious relationship with senior management, since they also represent the interests of professionals. In universities, middle managers occupy the positions of head of department, or dean of faculty (a larger administrative grouping). In schools, they are subject or year heads. In hospitals, they are the bridge between general managers and medical or nursing staff.

In large organisations, there are also a large number of administrators and technical support staff. In universities, for example, each academic department has traditionally had a departmental secretary (more usually a small team of administrators) who is responsible for record keeping and coordinating the activities of lecturers. In addition, there will be technical specialists, providing services to managers. Although it is hard to obtain figures, a considerable number of new positions have been created since the 1980s that are directly or indirectly concerned with measuring and assuring performance. Examples are statisticians employed to collect and analyse performance data in hospitals and police forces. Public sector organisations also advertise many positions in quality assurance. These employees develop and maintain the quality assurance policies required by outside bodies, and collect information for use in internal audits or external inspections.

It is not always possible to estimate the numbers of managers and administrators working in the public sector or their ratio to professional staff, partly because the roles overlap. The size of the public services, and the proportion of managers, grew during the 1980s despite the commitment of Margaret Thatcher's government to reduce the state (Wilding, 1992). It has also grown substantially under New Labour, particularly in health, education, transport and the criminal justice system.[2] To some extent, the rise of quality assurance as a management tool committed to providing better value for money, and even programmes of privatisation, masks an expansion of the numbers employed directly or indirectly through taxation. This is perhaps inevitable, given that Britain is a post-industrial economy in which most of the population either works in service industries or is employed by the state.

Quality assurance in universities

One aspiration behind writing this text, which is influenced by interpretive sociological traditions such as symbolic interactionism and ethnomethodology, has been to ground the general literature on managerialism, which primarily lists and evaluates government initiatives, with concrete observations of people engaged in actual activities. This section describes some aspects of how quality assurance operates in two contemporary universities: university A, which is a university college, oriented towards teaching, that has aspirations to become a university in Britain, and university B, which is a medium-sized Australian university.[3] In the case of university A, the emphasis is on the system of quality assurance during the 1990s. In the case of university B, the focus is on describing procedures employed in the early 2000s.

To pre-empt the criticism that writing about what is taking place around you is too easy to do or somehow not real research, it is worth noting that in the interpretive tradition there can be no stronger data than what is observed on the basis of close and intimate familiarity with a social setting or occupational group over a period of years. As Gouldner (1971), Bourdieu (1990) and others have eloquently noted, intellectuals have nothing to be ashamed of in reflecting on their own place in society. Universities are central institutions in the modern world, and the changes that are taking place there have understandably generated much comment and reflection. In Garfinkel and Wieder's (1991) terms, they provide a 'perspicuous setting' for studying quality assurance.

In terms of the wider institutional context, there has been a successful drive to expand the higher education system in each country, so that all universities are required to take on students who would, in previous years, not have attended university. There is, therefore, a contradiction between the objective of increasing participation and maintaining standards that often surfaces in debates about public services. British universities face penalties for not increasing student numbers, but can also be exposed in inspections by the Quality Assurance Agency for Higher Education (QAA) for poor marking practices. In general terms, however, the pursuit of quality is no longer seen as an aspiration for excellence. Governments are committed to increasing participation as an international measure of national success and standing, and everyone knows that to achieve this requires changing both the content of the curriculum and methods of teaching. Quality assurance cannot be separated from this wider process of reform, and is often used as an instrument to achieve changes necessary for the expansion of higher education. These contradictions can be seen when one considers different measures of quality in universities, such as assessment, feedback forms, annual monitoring, accreditation and external inspections.

Assessment

One measure of quality in universities is the outcomes achieved for students, which are measured in terms of degree passes and classes of degree. There is a tendency by governments to present these as objective measures. Education ministers in Britain announce each year on the publication of A-level results that educational standards are rising, and they sometimes make similar claims about the increased numbers graduating from universities. The problem with these claims is that standards can be changed to produce academic achievement. There have been criticisms in recent years that pressures to recruit more students, with lower levels of ability, have led to a decline in standards. It is also alleged that there has been more general grade inflation, so students who would previously have been considered weak or 'less academic' are not simply passing but obtaining upper seconds.

Standards can be reduced in many and various ways, for example, simply by removing a difficult course from the curriculum. In university A, there was an elaborate process of second marking and moderation by an external examiner to ensure that standards were maintained. However, many people complained that the power of external examiners was being gradually reduced in examination boards, and administrative rules made it difficult for students to fail courses. In university B, following a practice that is common in Australia and North America, objective marks were converted into a set distribution, so that a percentage of students received high marks whatever the actual standard, preventing comparisons with other courses or how a different cohort performed the previous year.

However they are processed, numerical grades obtained on courses are regarded as an objective measure of performance. The student goes away with a classification or set of transcripts that can be compared with those of students in other institutions (even if the actual standard is quite different). The university also has a set of figures that represents its own performance in relation to other institutions. One can argue that these figures are, at the very least, potentially misleading, since a lot depends on the criteria applied at different stages of the assessment process, which can differ between markers or institutions. Nevertheless, this remains an important way in which universities are assessed and allocated funding by central government.

Feedback forms

Another measure that concerns lecturers and managers in universities is not how well students perform in assessments, but whether they are satisfied with their courses (now often called 'units' or 'modules'). This information is now collected in educational institutions across the world by giving feedback forms to students. Although staff and students are rarely satisfied with how they are used to measure or assure quality, these forms have become a taken-for-granted part of higher education. Little is known about the circumstances that led to the introduction of forms in British universities. Australian universities faced pressure to introduce them during the 1980s when Commonwealth funding was made conditional on investing in quality assurance procedures.

A great deal of time and money is now spent collecting information on student satisfaction. Some larger universities employ units of three or four full-time staff to design and administer forms, and conferences are held entirely devoted to discussion of how to obtain and analyse feedback. In university B, there were regular reviews designed to improve and develop the system. One new initiative was a requirement that lecturers tell students the changes made as a result of last year's feedback, thereby demonstrating that suggestions were taken seriously. This is an example of how the basic assumption behind quality assurance, that there is a continuous cycle of improvement, is built into procedures for measuring quality.

In university A, summary scores from feedback forms, along with a 'module report' prepared by the lecturer, were reviewed by line managers so that, if problems were evident, these could be discussed at annual appraisal meetings. In university B, the scores were also made available on a website. The thinking behind this was that students as consumers could choose courses that were graded highly. This can be contrasted with the professional view, discussed in Chapter Three, that the client does not always know best.[4]

Finally, it is worth noting that many universities also obtain feedback from student representatives. Committees of this kind met several times each year in university A to address general issues of concern, such as library provision or problems arising from the allocation of scarce resources such as car parking, but also as an opportunity to discuss differences of perspective between students and lecturers on courses. In university B, there were fewer meetings of this kind, and it often proved difficult to recruit representatives. In each university, feedback forms were viewed as a more reliable measure of quality since they canvassed a wider range of opinion. It was accepted that it was not possible to satisfy everyone, and that in the end this was a professional judgement made by the lecturer. However, feedback forms and student representatives were required for quality assurance purposes: this is one system or procedure that external inspectors examined when reviewing universities.

Annual monitoring

Examination and coursework results and student feedback form two elements of an integrated system of quality assurance in universities that is examined by outside assessors. It would be a mistake, however, to see quality as something that is simply the concern of an external agency. Instead, in public sector institutions like universities there is an emphasis on writing about, and reflecting on, achievement at all levels of the organisation. There are various ways in which this is done and it is worth contrasting procedures in universities A and B.

University A

The performance review system in this institution was called 'annual monitoring'. This started after examinations when 'field chairs', academics responsible for managing subject-based groups, were sent blank reports for each course or 'module' taught by their fields. The reports contained statistical information of the distribution of marks and the mean achieved for the course, which in this university was viewed as an objective measure independently checked by second marking, and an external examiner who looked at a sample of examinations and coursework.[5] The reports asked lecturers to comment on the results, so, for example, if a cohort had done unusually well or badly, they were expected to provide an explanation. Attached to each report was a summary of the information obtained through student feedback forms. Lecturers were asked to comment on the scores obtained, and offer some explanation if these were lower than average. Finally, there was a section on the report where each lecturer was asked to explain any changes to the module for next year.[6]

Annual monitoring did not end when lecturers returned their reports on modules to field chairs. In September of each year, field chairs were asked to review the achievements and problems faced during the year. These reports also listed the means obtained in units, and explained any cases where there was a high failure rate.[7] Each field chair also had to attach an action plan listing a set of objectives to be reviewed the following year. In practice, this proved difficult to do.

**Figure 5.1: The annual monitoring process in university A
(a cycle of continuous improvement)**

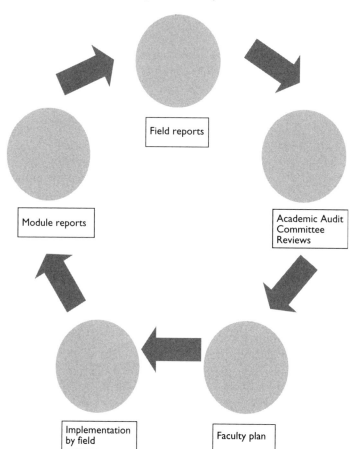

Field reports

Academic Audit
Committee
Reviews

Module reports

Implementation
by field

Faculty plan

Field chairs often had difficulty setting specific objectives that could be achieved within a year, so reports often stated the same objective from year to year (an example would be 'continue with school visits', with the aim of increasing recruitment).

Like other large organisations, universities have a number of tiers of management or organisational accountability. A key administrative unit in university A was the faculty that brought together a number of 'fields', which were grouped into 'departments'. The faculty also had a quality assurance role in relation to the different fields through the faculty board, a large committee comprising nominated representatives that met six times each year to review new courses and other business. In November of each year, this board met to consider the field reports that then became part of a faculty annual report to the university. These reports were circulated electronically and field chairs also spoke about the strategic issues raised by the reports at the meeting.

The quality assurance system in this university was, however, not simply an internal process of discussion and review within faculties. Each faculty also sent two representatives to the Academic Audit Committee that met regularly during the year. It produced independent reports about every faculty based on sending two representatives as internal reviewers. Their task was to review the reports at the main meeting and to comment on the effectiveness of the review process. This was accomplished by reading the reports, but also by attending or reading the minutes of faculty and field meetings.

University B

'Old' universities in the United Kingdom and elsewhere usually have fewer committee meetings, and a less elaborate system of quality assurance. In university B, there was no requirement for lecturers to review their courses formally each year, and no equivalent to produce annual reports for each administrative unit. There was, however, a system of periodic reviews in which members of other institutions examined internal reports and documents, and also had the opportunity to interview staff. Each school (the equivalent of a department in university A) was also encouraged, although not required, to have an advisory committee, in which representatives from the wider community and student representatives could review achievements during the past year, and the report from these committees became part of the university's annual quality review process. These committees were, however, mainly an opportunity to have a general discussion on strategic issues. There was no requirement for each member of staff to report detailed information on performance through the equivalent of fields, or for this information to be submitted as a formal report to the university.

The difference between these two institutions is worth mentioning, because quality assurance procedures are by no means uniform across institutions concerned with delivering the same kind of service. It could also be argued that quality assurance had been taken seriously in British 'new' universities, those former polytechnics that secured the university title in 1992, for some years and was not viewed as imposing an additional reporting burden. The political debate about quality assurance in higher education only arose when the government extended this regulatory mechanism to 'old' universities in the late

1990s. Some critics would probably be happy with a two-tier system, where only lower-tier universities are inspected.

Accreditation

At its widest, quality assurance involves far more than writing formal reports during the annual monitoring process, and has become built into the routine business of a university. One example of this is the care taken to document and check qualifications. This has always happened in recruiting new members of staff, but has also become important when appointing external examiners. It is often the case that a junior lecturer cannot examine a PhD thesis even if the academics involved believe that he or she is qualified: examinations are governed by quality assurance procedures devised by the university, which have to be followed without deviation.

PhD supervisors also have to show that they have the right qualifications, and undergo regular reaccreditation to demonstrate that they are still qualified. Doctors and nurses have been required by health authorities to take refresher courses for some years, although they have expressed concerns that the courses are not always useful or relevant to practice. In the case of university lecturers, it was once assumed that possession of a doctorate demonstrated a commitment to keeping up to date in that discipline. However, accreditation for graduate supervision has recently been introduced in many universities. This has partly arisen from a concern about completion rates, and a desire to avoid costly litigation that can arise from students who receive inadequate support or supervision.[8] However, it also stems from the belief that standards can be improved by sending staff on training courses.

At university A, all supervisors were encouraged to attend a training day in which a consultant explained the purpose of the PhD, and participants worked in small groups through case studies that illustrated what could go wrong (such as how to help students who suffered from health or financial problems, or had unrealistic expectations over the level of originality required). In later years, there was a compulsory programme of events, so supervisors had to attend two professional development seminars each year, in order to be allowed to continue supervising.[9] At university B, all supervisors, ranging from new members of staff to professors, were required to complete electronic forms to re-register. In any three-year period, they had either to attend training courses or complete a web-delivered course. This involved working through a number of case studies and exercises designed to encourage reflection on supervision. The accreditation process was subsequently made easier when it was possible to tick a box, stating that research relevant to the project had been conducted recently.

External inspections

In addition to these routine, internal measures of quality, British universities are also subject to external inspections. Academic staff are concerned with teaching students, conducting research, or in many cases a mixture of both. Unusually among public sector institutions, these two sides of practitioners' work are assessed separately. The QAA assesses the quality of teaching, and the Higher Education Funding Council for England (HEFCE) manages the Research Assessment Exercise (RAE) that has measured the quality of research since 1992.[10] Although everyone in universities is affected by these periodic external reviews, the majority of work falls on managers and administrative support staff. The QAA, for example, requires institutions to provide a large amount of documents to show that there are proper quality assurance policies and procedures.

At the end of the 1990s, before John Randall's resignation as Chief Executive of the QAA, there was a rolling programme of subject inspections, with visits to universities that involved observing lectures and tutorials. In addition, inspectors examined reading lists, sample essays and examination scripts, and external examiners' reports for particular courses. Preparing for an inspection in university A was a lengthy process involving numerous meetings, the creation of new administrative posts and briefings for relevant staff.[11] Minutes of relevant meetings at faculty, departmental and field level had to be organised in date order, so that inspectors could track actions taken to address targets set in the previous year's annual monitoring report and related faculty and departmental plans. When QAA inspections involved visits, these and other documents, carefully indexed in 30 or so colour-coded lever-arch files, were placed in an operations room to enable inspectors to check information they collected through interviewing staff and students against the official or documentary version of the university's problems and achievements.

The files themselves represented months of work preparing for an inspection. Delegated staff spent many hours working through the checklists provided by inspectors, identifying potential problems and taking remedial action. Senior managers led this process, and it was also arguably their own managerial work that was being inspected, as much as how courses were delivered on the ground. During the visit itself, they greeted the inspectors on behalf of the institution. They also had the opportunity to respond to the preliminary findings at a face-to-face meeting.

Managers also played a major part in organising and directing this university's response to the RAE. In simple terms, this invited universities to submit groups of staff for assessment, and their publications were then evaluated by an expert panel. Before making any decisions, however, universities needed to know what individual researchers were doing, so a great deal of time was spent by administrators in collecting this information. There was considerable scope for universities to make strategic decisions in preparing for the RAE, such as supporting particular areas or making appointments. Academics in a particular subject area were, of course, to some extent involved in these decisions and in writing the contextual statement presenting a department in a good light, but the key strategic decisions were made by managers. One can, therefore, see in each of these areas, how external inspection created administrative work. Certainly the biggest growth area in universities, as in other public sector organisations, has been managerial and clerical staff. In university A, over 50 per cent of office space was given to administrators, which is common in many British 'new' universities.[12]

Quality assurance in a police force

The next chapter will examine responses from professionals to the introduction of quality assurance procedures and systems. However, before doing so, it is worth looking, for comparative purposes, at quality procedures in another public sector agency. While considering different avenues to pursue in this study, permission was obtained to interview quality assurance managers working in a British police force.[13] Although this is very much an outsider's account, it provides another example of how public sector management has developed. The following summary describes some aspects of internal inspection (the equivalent of annual monitoring in universities). The police force was also inspected by three external inspection agencies, forming a cross-cutting system of accountability in the period 2002-03.

Internal inspection

Police forces are large organisations, and this force comprised ten areas or Basic Command Units (BCUs), the largest of which employed several hundred officers. This police force took internal inspection seriously, and had developed a system, only formalised in the late 1990s, in which each BCU was inspected twice a year. A team of seven was responsible for arranging the visits and preparing reports, comprising two civilian auditors, two inspectors, a part-time crime auditor and a systems auditor, who concentrated on the Police National Computer. The manager of the unit wrote up the reports. The procedures employed in analysing documents and conducting 'reality checks' were based on a model used by Her Majesty's Inspectorate of Constabulary (HMIC) called 'Going Local'. There were two stages of assessment, each involving visits to the area:

> 'It starts with a desk top assessment, I suppose, and document collection. The inspectors come to the police areas and collect all the information, look at some of the performance results, and then you go to the area, conduct the reality check and we produce an inspection report and performance information pack for that area.'

There were six areas covered by a report: how the force was managed; its own systems for performance management; use of intelligence; processes in customer management and crime management; handling of major incidents; and the system of financial management. The auditors then met the area commander, and worked through the report, ensuring that he or she was happy with the conclusions. This was not, however, the end of the process:

> 'The process finishes off with what we call an ACC inspection. The Assistant Chief Constable responsible for that area takes this report and visits the police area for a full day. He will sit down with the Area Command Team in the morning and work through the document. He will also have focus groups with various members of staff, talk to one or two selected people, provide feedback for the command team, and finish it off with an appraisal for the area commander.'

The reports from these inspections were large documents that recorded different aspects of performance in some detail with charts and tables. They were intended principally for senior managers, and were not generally available through the force, to encourage officers to be frank in their comments. In addition, the unit carried out inspections of support departments, such as control rooms, and thematic inspections across the force, for example on how officers used firearms.

Best Value inspection

Best Value inspections were established by the 1999 Local Government Act with the objective of improving the performance of management across local government. They were not strictly speaking inspections in the sense of an assessment by an external agency. Instead, they were a requirement for public agencies to conduct reviews of their own systems and procedures. When the interviews for this study were being conducted, Best Value was being phased out in this police force, and overtaken by HMIC baseline inspections. However, for a number of years it had been part of the regulatory environment for this police force.

Prior to 1999, this police force had already employed the European Excellence Model as a quality tool in thinking about quality processes. This had started when civilian managers had been introduced into the police; they had looked around industry and adapted it for their purposes. Best Value was intended to institutionalise this reflective review process, based on devising and measuring performance indicators, and conducting thorough reviews across areas of performance. This police force had already conducted 18 reviews:

> 'We're now in year five of the programme, and in the first two years we did what's called a corporate assessment, basically what are the strengths and weaknesses around a number of issues. And at that time call handling, volume crime, sickness management were all issues that were perceived to be areas where we needed to improve by some margin. We had a probably overly ambitious review programme and we decided to look at those key areas first.'

The aim of a Best Value review was to make continuous improvement a reality by measuring the extent of a problem, identifying possible causes, taking measures to address these and following this through with further measurement. As in the case of internal inspections, this involved analysing documents and conducting focus groups with officers to check what was happening on the ground (the term often used by managers is 'drilling down'). The police force had, for example, conducted a successful review of sickness management that had reduced sickness by 20 per cent. It would appear that, in this case, it was not difficult to identify the problem or solution; the challenge lay in encouraging local managers to follow standard procedures and keep proper records. The review team had discovered, to begin with, that the force had no written sickness policy, so local managers had no guidance and were under no pressure to address high levels of sickness. There were also inadequate procedures for measuring the extent of the problem:

Q: How did you reduce the sickness rate?

A: I would say that in all the BV reviews we have done, we have found that the performance management information that we collect either isn't accurate or valid, and on sickness management we found that we were severely under-reporting. So that was an issue in itself.... Some of it is administrative error. A good example is someone's been off for three months, but when they come back it says six weeks.... For one thing there were no return-to-work interviews being done. The first question on the form is when did you return to work, so you get some key triggers in there. We found that personnel managers were not actually doing visits to the homes. There were issues on was this a genuine case of sickness or was it work-related or not, or was it physical or a case of stress.... So basically poor control. I wouldn't say it was seen as unimportant, but now sickness is taken very seriously. It's managed very well. Then it wasn't really on the agenda. Well, the one thing we can control [in the police] is the productivity of our staff. Unlike in a business you can't go into the market and say, 'If you give us another x million pounds, we will do this for you'. You've got finite resources. Basically the review looked at two areas, carrot and stick really, we found there were patterns, and we found that the highest sickness was females in late 20s and 30s – children. We did not have any flexible working policies....

Best Value was being run down in the police, partly because it was felt that local managers were reviewing their activities without the need for this to be formalised. At its height, when nine reviews were being conducted annually, this police force had spent £3-£4 million annually, mainly on salary costs for review teams. This had been scaled down to £75,000, although the interviewee knew of police forces of a similar size that still had seven people at a cost of £350,000 working on Best Value reviews.

Baseline inspection

HMIC conducted periodic inspections of the different BCU areas in this police force, known as baseline inspections. These took place less frequently than internal inspections: each BCU might be inspected every three years. According to some quality managers, they were also less detailed than either internal or Best Value inspections:

> A1: If you're comparing internal inspections to HMI, I would say we are more in-depth and thorough in that we take a longer time to do it, probably have more people involved in the inspection process.

> A2: The force assessment may seem most dramatic but I would suggest it is the lightest touch because it is based on self-assessment. There are 300 questions you have to answer so it is self-assessment plus a series of semi-structured interviews.

Although managers in the BCU had to answer 300 questions, it was suggested that these only required short answers, and the inspectorate did not seek to challenge the self-assessment of managers in the same way as internal inspections. Reading between the lines, one can see that the principal difference lies in the fact HMIC inspection reports were available to the public and allowed comparison between police forces. Even though the internal and HMIC inspectors were looking at the same thing, there was no guarantee that they would reach the same conclusions. Interestingly, the performance data collected from internal inspections or from Best Value reviews did not appear in the HMIC report, even though HMIC conducted their own thematic inspection of performance management across the police force. It had also recently taken over the responsibilities of the Audit Commission in conducting inspections (involving documentary analysis and interviews with the research team) of a sample of Best Value reviews conducted each year.[14]

Crime recording

Although all these inspection reports were partly based on 'reality check' interviews with managers and other staff, the most striking feature is pages of tables showing performance in numerical terms. BCUs were, for example, assessed in terms of crime rates, or the amount of calls processed each year for different categories of offence. The

Home Office has been concerned in recent years, through the establishment of the Police Standards Unit, with improving the reliability and comparability of this performance data. For this reason, it commissioned the Audit Commission to conduct an annual inspection of data collection procedures. This has resulted in a national report grading each BCU on how accurately it records crime.

Some insight into the work involved in this aspect of quality assurance as it affects policing can be obtained from an interview conducted at the local District Audit Office with an auditor who had conducted the first of these inspections. This was a national audit, so local auditors followed working papers and guidelines disseminated by a regional coordinator. The methodology involved sitting in police stations and checking how crimes should be recorded according to the national standard against how they were actually recorded. The amount of work was considerable:

> 'When it came to looking at the incident record, we had 2,800 incident records to look at. We did it over three-and-a-half weeks. We had one of our performance specialists, and we also had police specialists who were normally police officers who were no longer in the service, who were able to look at things. For example, if I looked at something, I might think that this should be a crime, but they would know with their knowledge of the law that it was an offence but not a crime. So they could help us with the finer definitions. But it was still a case of going through every single one and saying how has this been closed, and tracing them all back to the incident records.'

To ensure consistency, the regional coordinator looked through every single review (a day's work going through three box files). The end result was not that national statistics could be seen as reliable, but that the error rates were known:

> 'If you have found very poor compliance with the standard, next year the force will have an awful lot more checking and work done with it than a force that has done very well. But even a force that has done well will have areas for improvement. In police force X, they have developed an action plan to address the issues which I said need improving. I will monitor how they achieve that as part of my ongoing audit. So with this process, they come out

Figure 5.2: Multiple and overlapping inspections in a police force

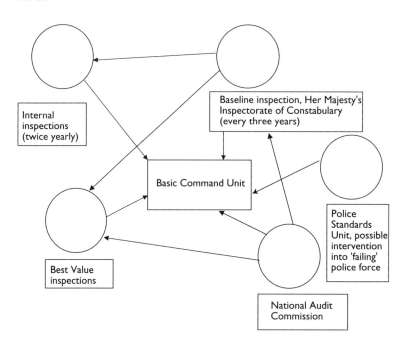

with an improvement plan, and that should help you move forward to develop, to deliver an improvement in services.'

The force itself also conducted its own monitoring of data collection policies, and contributed to discussions led by the Police Standards Unit. In addition to a team of officers and civilian staff responsible for internal inspection, Best Value and baseline inspections, and cross-checking inspections, there were three staff concerned with statistics and data quality. At the time of the interviews for this study, they were, for example, engaged in assessing and providing feedback to the national comparisons published in the form of 'spidergrams' by the Police Standards Unit. This was an attempt to compare 'families of forces', and so avoid the usual misleading characteristics of league tables. Although this account of quality assurance in a police force by no means addresses all its concerns and activities, one can see how a large group of managerial and administrative staff were involved, and that much of this work was concerned with making performance accountable to external bodies.

The costs of quality

This short outline of quality assurance procedures and systems in universities and a police force illustrates the large amount of work taking place at an organisational level in monitoring and assessing quality. Chapter Three considered the objections of professionals to these developments, suggesting that inspection implies a lack of trust in their competence or commitment to helping clients. In this chapter, it seems appropriate to consider how managers understand their relationship with the professionals they manage. This chapter argues that management, as a professional occupation, itself involves taking a moral stance of knowing better than professionals what is good for the organisation, and therefore for the services provided to the public. At the same time, managers are trying to protect professionals and themselves from what they see as excessive, and badly thought-out, regulation.

Managing professionals

Writing about work and organisations is always, inherently, political in that powerful groups have a vested interest in defining the world in their own terms. Marxist and other leftist writers will portray any industrial or public sector enterprise as riven by suppressed or actual conflict. Many have suggested, applying Braverman's (1974) ideas, that professionals always face a process of deskilling as organisations seek to exploit their labour most effectively. By contrast, Taylor (1990) argued that workers should defer to management experts who are best placed to keep them in work. Later management theorists, such as Deming, have argued that the diverse groups making up a private company or public organisation share the same objectives and values, and should all be involved in decision making.

Sociologists writing on management and the professions have also suggested that it is a mistake to see them as opposing camps with separate values. Many of the contributors to Exworthy and Halford (1999) point out that, in any large public sector organisation, the managers are also usually professionals. Freidson (1984) has argued that there has been a complex restratification, so that professionals are increasingly managed by other professionals. Nevertheless, there is still clearly a difference in perspective, in that becoming a senior manager and to some extent a middle manager may require having to make difficult decisions, for example in making staff redundant or pursuing a programme of restructuring with the aim of improving productivity. The distrust and suspicion felt by many professionals towards senior managers, if not middle managers who share their values and interests, is certainly evident in universities, schools and hospitals, even though it usually takes the form of grumbling, rather than attempts through the unions to curb management power. How, though, do managers view professionals?

The process of socialisation involved in becoming a manager at different levels of an organisation has not so far been studied.[15] There have, however, been many studies of how professionals acquire a particular set of values and outlook through formal training courses, and informally from working in different occupational settings (for example, Becker et al, 1961; Skolnick, 1967; Atkinson, 1997). There are many routes into management, and it is not professionalised in the sense of new recruits having to learn a particular body of knowledge.[16]

Given that senior managers have to portray organisations as positively moving forward while committed to common goals, they do not usually reflect publicly on internal conflicts or differences in perspective. The distance between the worlds of front-line staff and senior management was, however, apparent from an interview conducted with a nurse who became a quality manager in a large teaching hospital (many administrators in hospitals are ex-nurses):

> 'There's a different language. I think the benefit you have if you're a nurse and have gone up through the ranks is that you have an understanding of what the world is like at ward level. It's not an organised world, it's a chaotic world. We've just been doing something called a piece inspection, and you walk on wards, and you see things and you think, "Well, surely that should be easy to sort out". But the world in which you work on a ward is very chaotic....You don't exist in a Monday-to-Friday lifestyle, you have a completely different routine in terms of the way you work.'

This interviewee also suggested that there is a class differential between nurses and patients in the wards (almost presented as the shopfloor in a factory) and professional managers, and even doctors, who are unable to communicate at this level:

> 'If you're a general manager who's gone through university, gone on the NHS training scheme, you've always been treated politely....You're probably most of the time having good interactions with people, because they recognise you

have influence and power even when you are relatively junior. It's quite different at ward level.... I mean the classic case is when the doctor does his ward rounds and then afterwards as a charge nurse I'd go round and interpret what the doctor had just said. This has to do culturally with where nurses come from.'

The hospital is perhaps an unusual case, because normally managers in public sector organisations have similar backgrounds to the people they manage. However, in any organisation managers will acquire a different outlook from attending training courses, informal socialisation with other managers, or simply being responsible for performance. To give another example from this hospital, the doctors inevitably wanted, on professional grounds, to prescribe the best-quality drugs. The managers, however, inevitably had a different perspective. They were sympathetic to the problems of professionals delivering services, but also far more aware of the financial realities:

'One of the pains of the neck as a general manager is that the consultants will say the Royal College guidelines say X, Y, Z, but that's all they are, guidelines. There's a difference between a guideline and what is statute, or what the Department of Health says. The Royal College will set the gold standard, and as a clinical person you want the gold standard, but in a management position you have a limited resource. You're constantly having to make decisions: "Well, are we able to live with that risk and accept that risk, how do we manage it as best we can?". Because you can't have the gold standard in everything, there is not a bottomless budget, there isn't.'

Managers have, therefore, a significantly different attitude to professional work than doctors, teachers, university lecturers and police officers, since they are responsible for providing a service within budget. Most come to believe that quality assurance is an important, and valuable, side of delivering a service, and that it is important for organisations to be accountable to wider publics. Moreover, they also believe that this cannot be left to professionals. From the perspective of one civilian quality manager working for the police, quality assurance was an uphill struggle against professionals and managers in organisations that were not sufficiently concerned with monitoring or improving quality:

> 'Our force is extremely anti-inspections and internal inspectorates. I joined in 1994 and the previous year they had slung out the internal inspectorate. And what they introduced was self-inspection, which was to send out forms to area and say, "Fill it in yourself". Anecdotally, they used to be filled in in the back of cars on night shift. You know, tick, tick, tick [laughs].'

From this perspective, what practitioners believe on the ground is almost irrelevant to whether inspection is worth doing. One gets a strong sense that professionals and managers inhabit different social worlds from this extract from an interview with another police quality manager:

Q: Tell me about a recent HMIC inspection.

A: We had a thematic inspection on the PNC, police national computer, a few weeks ago. We sent them pre-prepared documents, and a schedule of interviews primarily. They like to do reality checks, focus groups. They will actually go and talk to constables and say, "How is it for you?". If you're out on the street and have your radio, how easy is it to contact PNC?

Q: So you think reality checks work?

A: Yes. If Best Value went, the one thing we would miss would be this kind of consultation.

Q: Do they welcome the opportunity to go on focus groups?

A: The constables? No, they're generally suspicious. They're obviously busy. What they want to know is: Is this going to affect me? Are you going to listen to what I say? Is it going to make a difference? It may not immediately.... And of course you will always get your barrack room lawyers, and people who have strong views. And you'll have as many other people who just haven't got a clue. They come and do a job and then they go home. And it's up to the management how they organise it.

There is no suggestion here that professionals are slack or incompetent. This interviewee appears to share the views of Taylor (1990), and other proponents of scientific management, that they do not have the scientific overview available to managers that enables an improvement in procedures that will benefit everyone. This makes for an interesting contrast to the professional perspective discussed in Chapter Three. Professionals, like doctors, teachers and lawyers, see themselves as knowing better than members of the public through having specialist expertise and being committed to service. Managers as another professional group see themselves as knowing better than professionals, and sometimes representing the public against professionals. There is, therefore, always potential for tension between them, even without restructuring imposed by government that leads to redundancies or 'work intensification'. At the same time, managers and administrators depend on the work of the professionals who deliver services, so one could argue that in practice police officers, nurses or university lecturers are largely left to manage their own work.

The demands of auditing and inspection

The next chapter examines the impact of quality assurance on professionals as part of discussion of the problem of 'red tape' in industrialised societies. Here it is worth noting that the group most immediately affected by these initiatives are managers. Managers undertake most of the work in conducting internal audits and preparing for external inspections, and many administrative jobs have been created by this new form of regulation. Managers also arguably have a greater emotional stake, both because they see themselves as responsible for the organisation (the manager's burden of responsibility) and because most of an inspection is concerned with assessing the standard of managerial work.

Although managers in the British public sector accept the need for quality assurance, they are critical of the excessive system of regulation, involving multiple cross-cutting inspections, that has developed to measure and assure quality. The police force used as an example in this chapter had made representations to simplify procedures to the Home Office. One manager, whose job involved trying to coordinate three overlapping inspections, described the present system as 'a nonsense' maintained by the reluctance of central government to merge HMIC, the Audit Commission and the new Police Standards Unit for 'political reasons'.

The large amount of time spent in preparing for external inspections was not perceived by this police force as adding anything to its own procedures of internal audit and inspection:[17]

Q: Do you trust or use their reports?

A: I don't personally, no. We read the bits that say we've got a really good internal inspection, obviously [laughs]. We pin that on the wall. No, our connection really with the external process is to make sure that we don't go trampling into an area when they're there. So, for example, when we've got an inspection planned and we find the HMI are coming in, we will just do a light touch or just a review of previous findings, something like that. We won't go into it in depth, because it would be unfair to be exposed to two sets of audits and inspections.

At the time of conducting this research, it is remarkable that findings by these agencies about different aspects of this police force were kept largely separate, even though some inspections were concerned with establishing that other inspections were accurate. Managers knew, of course, that there were good reasons for this level of duplication, and the system was even more complex than reported, since each report had to follow a complex trail through various external bodies including the Police Authority. This was not necessarily experienced as a burden, in the sense of how professionals complain about excessive paperwork, but it was seen as tying up management and administrative resources that could be put to better use.

Notes
[1] For two powerful critiques of the rise in white-collar and administrative work earlier in the 20th century, see Mills (1951) and Whyte (1956).

[2] To give an example, the 2002 Spending Review proposed employing 350,000 new staff across the public sector over the next three years.

[3] It would not take much detective work to identify these institutions, which are effective and successful in pursuing their respective missions. Many of the policies and procedures described in this chapter, and the organisational cultures around measurement and quality assurance, can be found across the British public sector.

[4] One problem identified in the Office of Public Services Reform (2003) review of inspectorates is that no one, outside a handful of senior managers, reads the reports posted on websites inevitably some weeks after the inspection. It was suggested that thought should be

given to using the media or other channels to communicate findings about, for example, schools or hospitals.

[5] The external examiner had an important role in quality assurance in this institution, writing an annual report on each module and on the degree as a whole.

[6] This report was intended to encourage lecturers to reflect on pedagogical issues. All too often, however, it was completed in a terse, almost ritualistic way. One lecturer always wrote for each course that the results were 'excellent' and the feedback 'positive'. Staff were sometimes encouraged by senior managers to expand on their problems and achievements, but only a few took advantage of this opportunity for professional development.

[7] The quality assurance system also required the distribution of marks to be discussed at a field meeting, and the minutes of this meeting attached to the annual monitoring report to demonstrate that the issue had been discussed. This is one example of how quality assurance imposes a reporting burden on practitioners. The real discussion had taken place informally earlier in the year, but this did not count for reporting purposes.

[8] There have been other shifts towards a model of PhD supervision based on industrial procedures. Whereas in previous decades, the organisation of supervision was left to academic staff, now the university requires annual reviews, monitored by the university Registry or research office. These require the supervisor, associate supervisor and postgraduate officer in a department to submit reports. Interestingly, the term 'signed off', which is used in government departments, is often used to describe successful PhD completions: they literally do have to be signed off by the various parties.

[9] At one seminar, the consultant even asked participants to complete feedback forms, which they dutifully did, even though many who attended were there effectively under duress.

[10] There have been changes to each type of assessment, just as any inspectorate has evolved in response to practical and political challenges. The aim in this chapter is not to give much detail on these changes, or

the political debates around, for example, concentrating 'scarce' resources in elite institutions (Roberts, 2005), but to describe some of the work involved.

[11] See Wiener (2000) for a detailed account of preparing for inspections in an American hospital.

[12] There is no discussion here of how university B was affected by external inspection. In Australia, there is no equivalent to the QAA inspection, although universities complain about over-regulation. The Research Quality Framework proposed in 2005, and likely to be implemented in 2008, is modelled on the British RAE.

[13] One reason the police force facilitated the research was because it was concerned about the burdens created by multiple inspections.

[14] It is worth noting that originally there was a separate Best Value Inspectorate. However, this was merged with the Audit Commission, partly to avoid duplicating inspections.

[15] The change that occurs on promotion to a managerial position, in terms of greater status and responsibility, but also no longer being able to fraternise with ordinary workers, has been a staple theme in fiction. See, for example, the account of Major Major's promotion in Joseph Heller's (1994) novel *Catch 22*.

[16] The management theorist Peter Drucker once suggested that management, like other fields of professional expertise, could not be learnt on training courses, which may also imply that performance cannot be measured.

[17] One could still argue that external inspection is a safety net for police forces that do not have their own internal systems.

SIX

The problem of red tape

Red tape as a social problem
- Classical perspectives on bureaucracy
- Contemporary debates
- Gouldner's constructionist approach

Complaints about quality assurance
- Academic malcontents
- Two interview studies

Experiencing everyday bureaucracy
- An ethics application
- Demonstrating quality in legal practice
- Accreditation: a nurse's tale
- Ticking the boxes
- A negative case study

Government initiatives to reduce red tape
- Regulating the regulators
- The Regulatory Impact Unit

The politics of red tape

Chapters Four and Five looked at quality assurance from the perspective of those committed to the goal of 'continuous improvement' in public sector work. Politicians and civil servants, government inspectorates concerned with quality assurance and managers in organisations all believe that professionals, if left to themselves, will not provide a satisfactory level of service to clients. They have to be made accountable through audit and inspection. This means that a large amount of managerial work inside organisations is concerned with collecting information about performance. The annual auditing cycle involves identifying problems, and making and implementing plans to achieve and demonstrate improvement. There may be problems with over-inspection, or overlapping systems of accountability, but, broadly speaking, both senior managers and the administrators who collect and analyse performance information genuinely believe that quality assurance is valuable and necessary, and can readily give examples of areas where improvement has been achieved or problems still need to be solved.

What, though, are the views of the professionals working in organisations affected by these changes? How have they responded to quality assurance initiatives? And how do they experience quality assurance in their day-to-day work? It has already been suggested that professionalism involves claiming to know what is best for clients, by virtue of acquiring specialist expertise and knowledge, so one might expect doctors or teachers to feel at least mildly irritated by calls for greater monitoring and regulation. This chapter approaches this topic from a different angle by considering complaints about excessive paperwork and 'red tape'. Since there may be readers looking for a straightforward critique of managerialism, it is worth stating from the outset that there is no suggestion that every professional shares these concerns, or that 'red tape' is an easy phenomenon to identify or describe. Instead, Alvin Gouldner's (1952) constructionist approach is adopted and developed in seeking to describe how it is experienced and comes to be seen as a social problem. Although scare quotes will not be used in the rest of this chapter, it should be remembered that 'red tape' is a lay concept, and, like 'managerialism', a pejorative term that is mainly used by critics of regulation.

The chapter starts by reviewing the criticisms made of bureaucracy by Max Weber and intellectuals with similar views, which seems important in view of the fact that many subsequent writers have cited Weber in support of their own arguments without always appreciating how they form part of a wider cultural critique of the modern world. It also reviews more recent debates between supporters and detractors of bureaucracy. It then considers Gouldner's suggestion that red tape does not exist as a problem that can be measured and identified using scientific methods, but is constructed through politically motivated definition and interpretation.

The chapter then considers some contemporary complaints about quality assurance as a form of bureaucracy, drawing on recent studies of doctors and teachers, and letters and opinion articles published by academics. It also looks at some candidate examples of red tape, focusing on the administrative work created by quality assurance as a new form of regulation affecting everyday life, and how this is experienced as burdensome. These include a negative and comparative example: to demonstrate that by no means everyone affected by these changes experiences them as problematic. The rest of the chapter considers the efforts of governments to combat red tape, and why these initiatives have had only limited impact on regulatory agencies.

Red tape as a social problem

The term red tape originates in 19th-century Britain as a complaint about interference in traditional rights and customs by central government (when official documents were literally tied up with red tape).[1] More recently, it has come to mean the delay and waste associated with large organisations where any request for action has to be properly documented and filed on the correct forms, and go through the correct channels with no room for local discretion. An example observed recently at an Australian police station is that someone reporting a crime had to supply three forms of identification, in two prescribed categories: the officer on reception could not take the matter further without having seen these documents, and apologised if this sounded like red tape.

One can see already how there may be good reasons for red tape, in that it might well be sensible for several officials to approve a requisition (not least because this reduces opportunities for corruption or fraud) or to check the identity of someone who might make a frivolous or vexatious complaint. Nevertheless, one can also see how some procedures might be viewed as burdensome, or result in frustration and delay. However, the complaints made by public figures and commentators in 19th-century Britain and later in 20th-century America were not simply directed at the inconvenience of waiting for a decision or completing an additional form, but also reflect deeper concerns about the growth of large-scale organisations and the modern state.

Classical perspectives on bureaucracy

Most citizens living in developed societies take the existence of a strong, sovereign state, providing services like health and education, and redistributing income through social security, largely for granted. The rise of the state in countries such as Britain happened gradually during the 19th century, partly as a response to the challenges of industrialisation and pressures for social programmes from democratic politics. The concept of citizenship where individuals accept financial responsibilities towards complete strangers through paying taxes to a national government in return for protection from disease and poverty is one of the great achievements of modernity.

Since it would almost be unthinkable to imagine civilised existence without large publicly funded bureaucracies such as the National Health Service, it requires some degree of historical imagination to appreciate why the political commentator Alexis de Tocqueville, writing at the start of the 19th century, and later sociologists and political scientists such as Roberto Michels were highly suspicious towards the modern state. To some extent, Michels and De Tocqueville were conservative thinkers, ambivalent or opposed to mass democratic societies, in which elites lost their privileges and status. De Tocqueville (2003) argued that the supposed freedom obtained through democratic revolutions was sham or illusory: there was no need for individuals to engage in critical thought or take democracy seriously in affluent societies where they were supported by state agencies and institutions from cradle to grave.

This is also, arguably, the right way to read Weber. In some respects, he was a great admirer of bureaucracy. He compliments it for allowing 'precision, speed, unambiguity, knowledge of the files, continuity, discretion, unity, strict subordination, reduction of friction and of material and personal costs' when compared with earlier 'collegial, honorific or avocational forms of administration' (Weber, 1991, p 214). At the same time, he is resigned rather than celebratory about bureaucracy, suggesting that 'the idea of eliminating these organisations becomes more and more utopian' now that 'the material fate of the masses depends upon the steady and correct functioning' of large organisations (Weber, 1991, p 229). Like De Tocqueville, and many 20th-century intellectuals, Weber was ambivalent about the progress achieved by industrialisation and the rise of the state. In complaining that the fate of the individual was to be a cog in the machine, he was partly talking about the growth of bureaucratic organisation in Bismark's Germany. He was also identifying a more general problem about the quality of human life in an over-regulated and rationalised society.

Contemporary debates

Debates among intellectuals about red tape during the 20th century have tended to have an ideological flavour. Liberals and leftists have generally found little to complain about in the growth of the state and the extension of regulation into new areas of social life, supported by taxing industry and commerce. Conservatives, on the other hand, including neo-liberals in our own times, favour privatising public services, and lower levels of support for the poor or unemployed. In some respects, this is a phoney war, in that to achieve political power in a democracy, it is necessary to obtain votes from the middle classes, many of whom are employed by the state. Public spending has increased under all governments, including those committed to neo-liberal reforms. At the time of writing, the Conservative opposition in Britain regularly criticises the Labour government for increasing bureaucracy, and it is claimed that thousands, if not tens of thousands, of civil service posts have been created since 1997. No political party could, however, win power by promising drastic cuts in the National Health Service or welfare state.

There have also, however, been some thoughtful contributions to the Weberian tradition that recognise the value of bureaucracy as a means of delivering public services while recognising its faults. Robert Merton argued during the 1940s that bureaucratic structures can result in a 'displacement of goals' so that officials follow rules even when these result in delay or inefficiency:

> This emphasis, resulting from the displacement of the original goals, develops into rigidities and an inability to adjust readily. Formalism, even ritualism, ensues with an unchallenged insistence upon punctilious adherence to formalized procedures. This may be exaggerated to the point where primary concern with conformity to the rules interferes with the achievement of the purposes of the organisation, in which case we have the familiar phenomenon of the technicism or red tape of the official. (Merton, 1952, p 366)

As recently as the 1970s, a number of academic commentators in America were advancing similar criticisms of bureaucracy. At the same time, articles complaining about the failings of government agencies regularly appeared in the media, and were well received by a large constituency that had suffered from insensitive treatment by bureaucracy ('petty bureaucracy' as it is sometimes called). Since then, there has been something of a fightback, with public administrators arguing that the complaints have been exaggerated and stirred up by ideologically motivated opponents.[2] Charles Goodsell (1983) has, for example, argued that those arguing against bureaucracy usually supply no empirical evidence. Drawing on a number of surveys, he shows how 'most citizens ... perceive far more good than bad in their daily interactions with it' (Goodsell, 1983, p 139).[3] Similarly, Paul du Gay (2000) has criticised both managerialist and romantic leftist critics, and argued that instead of undermining bureaucracy, we should appreciate it as making a valuable contribution to a liberal, democratic society.

Gouldner's constructionist approach

If government is generally efficient and benign, why do people complain about bureaucracy and red tape? Arguably the most interesting contribution to the literature on red tape is an essay by Alvin Gouldner anticipating the constructionist approach to social problems that became popular during the 1970s. Gouldner asked, 'why is it ... that the very same procedures or practices which one group may characterize as red tape may be viewed by another group as deserving no invidious label?' (Gouldner, 1952, p 411). He argued that those most likely to complain were conservatives whose interests were threatened by the redistributive state.

Gouldner also recognised, however, that complaints about red tape were more widespread, and reflected 'the objective attributes of the situation with which [the individual] comes into contact' (Gouldner, 1952, p 411). In the article, he explored different dimensions of dissatisfaction with bureaucracy through analysing interviews conducted with 124 respondents, and also group interviews (in today's terminology, focus groups).[4] He found that many respondents (and not just those with conservative political views) felt powerless when dealing with large organisations. They also resented being treated as an object (a 'case'), and the fact that they had to give private information to strangers. Gouldner, therefore, concluded that there was some truth to the 'red-tape stereotype', but that when people complained about bureaucracy they were expressing a more general disquiet or resentment about mass, industrialised society.[5]

Complaints about quality assurance

Quality assurance is not the same phenomenon as red tape, and indeed the quality movement in government has sought to address consumer dissatisfaction about impersonal and ineffective bureaucracy through introducing feedback forms and attempting to improve performance. There are, however, some common features, not least that people have different views about the value of this new form of regulation. Managers and quality assurers see it as beneficial for society, whereas many professionals view it as either unnecessary or harmful. The critics also often describe quality assurance as a form of red tape: one that slows down organisations through creating burdensome and unnecessary work. This section will document some of these complaints, considering first the special case of academics who have been more vocal than other public service professionals in resisting what they describe as managerialism. As will become clear later in the chapter, not all professionals share these views, although many do see quality assurance as burdensome and unnecessary (one way of defining red tape). The main concern here is not, however, to make a case about numbers and representativeness, but to explore what seems to be at issue when public sector professionals complain about quality assurance.

Academic malcontents

It is perhaps unsurprising that university academics, who have more time for reflection and professional development than many occupations, have been most vocal in complaining about quality assurance initiatives, at least in the weekly *Times Higher Education Supplement* (THES). One rarely finds the issue of red tape or managerialism mentioned in *Nursing Times*, the *General Practitioner* or *Law Society Gazette*. There has, however, been at least one critical article in most issues of THES about the Quality Assurance Agency for Higher Education (the QAA), the Research Assessment Exercise, or the failings of university managers for many years.

Extracts from two articles will be enough to convey the flavour of these comments. The first is a piece by a newly retired academic reflecting on his experience of quality assurance. He complained that as a professor in an education department he had been subject to inspections by the schools inspectorate Ofsted for six out of the past seven years. In a two-year period, his school 'had Ofsted, the Quality Assurance Agency, the research assessment exercise, an internal audit, a financial review, and many other semi-formal appraisals' (Wragg, 2003). He notes that, having retired, things have improved:

> Instead of writing only early in the morning, after 5pm and at weekends, I am now creative during the day. I teach without a faceless bloke-with-clipboard at the back of the lecture room. No business plan, no utopian mission statement. I cannot remember a single statement from any plan I have ever read. Worse, I cannot remember one from any plan I have written. (Wragg, 2003)

The second is a news report about a university lecturer who retired in mid-career to breed greyhound dogs. After going into education because she loved teaching, she found that the workload increased, and she had to reduce the time spent on each student. She also made some observations about the growing emphasis on quality assurance in teaching and research:

> The amount of time that you spend being prepared to be measured, being measured and recovering from being measured detracts so much from the job in hand....Research is just about doing the kind of work that your institution thinks will work in the research assessment exercise, not about the serious pursuit of knowledge. (Baty, 2004)

Each of these retiring academics makes the ideological point that professionals are no longer trusted, and it also seems evident they are unhappy about increased workloads and declining standards in a period of expansion in higher education. However, it is also worth noting that what Goulder called the 'objective attributes' of red tape appear to be central in these complaints. They are complaining that time spent on teaching and research is eaten into by administration related to quality assurance. This includes attending meetings, filling in forms and writing mission statements and policy documents. These systems and procedures are portrayed as burdensome and unnecessary, one definition of red tape.

Two interview studies

There have been several surveys, often funded by unions, about the plight of public sector workers such as nurses, doctors and teachers. These show that workloads have increased dramatically while salaries have fallen relative to other occupational groups. Few researchers have asked professionals about issues relating to quality assurance, although two British studies are worth reporting: by Stephen Harrison and George Dowswell (2002) on general practitioners and by Hilary Sommerlad (1999, 2001) on legal aid lawyers. They are each critical towards the new public management, and believe that it leads to a lower level of service for clients, through reducing professional independence and discretion. Another theme is the restructuring of professions into highly paid managers and insecure and deskilled workers, a version of the influential argument advanced by Harry Braverman (1974) about the labour process in capitalist societies.

This literature is discussed in the next chapter, but for now it is worth noting that only a few of the professionals interviewed for these studies express their criticisms of quality assurance initiatives in precisely these terms. There is also some evidence that they see themselves as fighting a losing battle against colleagues who see nothing wrong with the new public management, and believe that these initiatives will improve quality in the public sector. The interviews do suggest, however, that many professionals feel burdened by the work involved in quality assurance. They believe either that it has no value in improving or maintaining quality, or that it can result in a reduction of quality through reducing the time available to do real work.

To give an example, one general practitioner complained about the requirement to write reports on 'clinical governance':

> 'It's all so time-consuming. All these things that they want you to do are just paper exercises. It's going to reduce time that you could be spending on patient care. The patients, as ordinary people, just want your time in the surgery, listening to them and addressing their needs. I don't think they'd like to think you were spending your time filling in forms and writing protocols for ridiculous things to keep somebody, somewhere happy. It's not enough to be doing all of these things, because in this practice we were doing pretty much everything that they want us to do, but you have to be supplying written, documentary evidence that you are doing it. I just think that's a waste of time.' (Harrison and Dowswell, 2002, p 214)

The claim here is that quality assurance takes a great deal of time in addition to normal work without adding anything in terms of improving quality. It is seen as 'ridiculous' or 'a waste of time'. The complaint about having to keep 'somebody, somewhere happy' is reminiscent of concerns in the bureaucracy literature about 'faceless' officials, and the powerlessness felt in dealing with large impersonal organisations. The solicitors interviewed by Sommerlad also complained about distant managers in the Legal Aid Board (LAB) (never described by their first names), and reported that maintaining the quality systems required to obtain a franchise took up time that would previously have been used in seeing clients:

> 'The administrative and management burden is appalling and increasing all the time as the LAB pushes more and more of it onto us ... producing the forms, that sort of thing. I'm the franchise person so I've had meetings with every team – that's 10 meetings – to see we're up to scratch with the franchising criteria – that's at least one to two

hours per meeting. Then they all have to go away and think about what I've said, consider their systems, whether they're franchise compliant, and work on them as a team. Then there's the burden on each individual solicitor ... the forms, extra letters and so so.... And they've changed the forms three times since last April ... so the old ones have to be rounded up and destroyed ... then there's the supervision requirements; I supervise five people, so I spend about 10 hours in formal supervision a month. It's overwhelming.' (Sommerlad, 2001, p 351)

This interviewee provides a good sense of how meetings are generated by a new system of regulation, and how regulatory agencies pass on administrative work to the organisations being regulated. The term 'colonisation' is used in this critical literature to suggest an alien force taking over the professions, and then inculcating or coercing workers into new values and practices, so they will be self-regulating.

At least one of the lawyers interviewed believed that the purpose of franchising was to save money by reducing the quality of service offered to clients, rather than to raise standards. One solicitor reported that she had been 'told by my boss that I could say what I had to say to clients much more briefly' and that 'my files were too good – there was too much client care'. This is another common complaint made by public sector professionals: that there is a disjunction between the rhetoric of continuous improvement and what is happening on the ground due to successive cutbacks.

Experiencing everyday bureaucracy

These studies are helpful in providing evidence that at least some professionals find quality assurance burdensome and unnecessary. They do not, however, supply much detail on how it is experienced as problematic in the course of day-to-day work. One difficulty is that, as often happens in interview studies, we are not given much ethnographic context. One of Sommerlad's interviewees (a manager in a large legal aid practice) described the work of managing a franchise as 'overwhelming' (Sommerlad, 2001, p 351). On the face of things, this suggests that the manager, personally, or the firm cannot keep up with the requirements made by the Legal Aid Board. It might, however, simply be a complaint that the firm needs full-time managers to organise the work, or a reflection of the interviewee's ideological distaste towards government cutbacks in legal aid.

The problem with interviews is not simply that they might report 'a set of idealised beliefs or post hoc rationalisations' (Sommerlad, 1999, p 312), but that it is very difficult when interviewing to obtain much insight into what people actually do at work. This creates a practical problem in that the only way to address the content of legal or medical practice is to obtain access as an ethnographer to a workplace. Harold Garfinkel and Lawrence Wieder have argued that this may not be enough, and the only way to capture and address the practical circumstances of the work is to become a competent practitioner, what they call the 'unique adequacy requirement of methods' (Garfinkel and Wieder, 1991).

The author's own experiences as a university lecturer can offer some insight into everyday bureaucracy and red tape in this particular professional field. In addition, interviews conducted with a few practitioners in different occupations provide more context and detail than simply the fact that these professionals object to not being trusted or are 'overwhelmed' with unnecessary paperwork. Two issues of particular interest are the amount of time spent on activities related to quality assurance, and what exactly is involved in completing 'routine' forms. Another area of interest is the pragmatic approach taken by professionals: red tape is a source of irritation but can be managed.

An ethics application

There are many new administrative demands caused by quality assurance initiatives in British universities, including the work involved in administering feedback forms and obtaining and renewing accreditation for PhD supervision, and the requirement to supply details of publications for the Research Assessment Exercise (RAE). Academics in Australia complain about similar procedures. None, however, takes up more time or is more resented, at least among those doing empirical research, than ethics review.

Ethics review was originally directed against abuses in the field of medical research, although it has been extended to any empirical research where there is a risk of harm being caused to 'human subjects'.[6] A central principle is that all research has to be reviewed by an ethics committee comprising academics (although not necessarily those with expertise in the application being reviewed) and representatives from the community. These committees have to ensure that research has scientific merit (so there is a quality assurance aspect) and that anyone participating in a research project understands the risks involved, and has given informed consent. This has usually been interpreted by ethics committees to mean that participants have to be supplied with an information sheet explaining possible risks, and that they are required to sign a consent form of the kind used in medical trials.

Submitting an ethics review is always a time-consuming process, particularly for someone new to the regulatory system. To feel confident enough to submit an application in Australia, the author attended a training course for potential reviewers, and spent several hours reading the national statements that set out the principles to be followed by ethics committees, and the local handbook for ethics applications in the relevant state. He has so far submitted two ethics applications (including one seeking permission to conduct interviews for this project), supervised several applications made by postgraduate students, and advised honours students on the procedures.[7]

To give an example of the administrative work involved, obtaining ethics clearance to conduct an observational study about the work of criminal justice professionals in children's courts involved drafting a 17-page application that provided background information about the project, identified the potential risks to research 'subjects' and explained how these could be reduced through securing 'informed consent'. Three consent forms were designed for different participants (magistrates, other practitioners and child defendants), an information sheet informing them about the potential risks, and a list of interview questions for practitioners. Owing to the risks involved in studying a vulnerable group, and the lack of familiarity of the regulators with ethnographic methods, the author was then asked to meet the ethics committee. The committee was particularly concerned that consent should also be obtained from the parents of child defendants. After this one-hour meeting, a revised application was submitted and approved, subject to making further minor changes to the consent forms and information sheets.

A year later, a progress report was requested, which required ticking boxes to confirm that no 'research subjects' had been harmed, and explaining any changes to the project. It also required giving details of any talks delivered about the project, and supplying copies of publications, presumably to check that the ethical procedures and guidelines had been followed. In total, preparing the original application, attending the meeting, revising the application and submitting this progress report took up almost two working days, that is, 16 hours of administrative work, two thirds of which was spent drafting the application and consent forms. If this research project had been conducted in Britain prior to 2005, none of this work would have been necessary.

It is now time to ask the question posed rhetorically by a police quality manager when describing overlapping forms of regulation by different inspectorates: is this bureaucracy? From the perspective of the regulator, there is a purpose to ethics review, and it is assumed that, over time, researchers will become used to completing applications and not find this burdensome. Most social scientists learn to live with ethics review in this way, although there are others who have principled (one might say 'ethical') objections to ethics review, on the grounds that it does more harm than good by discouraging research on 'sensitive' topics.[8] However, even researchers without ideological objections can become irritated or frustrated. This is partly because one is dealing with an impersonal bureaucracy where one has to follow set procedures, such as the fact that the name of a supervisor can only be changed on a PhD project by completing a form, and sending a signed copy clearly marked on the top of the form 'signed copy' to satisfy the external auditor. There is also the constant implication that researchers are not to be trusted: that without regulation, they will harm the people they are studying.

Demonstrating quality in legal practice

Sommerlad's (1999) study based on interviewing managers in legal aid practices indicated some discontent towards, and distrust of, the quality assurance initiatives administered by the Legal Aid Board (now the Legal Services Commission). This might be expected not only because levels of bureaucracy have increased, but also because the rates for legal work have been reduced, with the result that some practitioners have given up this area of work. Interviews were conducted for the present study with members of a law firm specialising in commercial fraud, where a large proportion of the work is funded through the Legal Services Commission. Interviews with those responsible for ensuring that the firm met its obligations revealed little sense that the franchise was regarded as 'overwhelming' or 'unworkable', although there was recognition that smaller firms could experience difficulties. The interviews did, however, reveal the amount of work involved in maintaining accreditation.

To ensure that its systems and procedures were in good shape in the event of an inspection visit, the firm had appointed a full-time administrator. This administrator had been a legal secretary, so this is an example of how regulation provides employment both for those conducting inspections and in the organisations being inspected, and new career routes for administrative staff. The objective was to provide an 'in-house check' so that 'when we are subject to an external audit, we can be reasonably comfortable that we are doing what we are meant to be doing, and doing that consistently'.

The principle behind franchising is that each firm can show that it has proper procedures and that an inspector can find documentary evidence that these are being followed:

> 'It's being able to show you have done various things, and the only way you can show them that you have the system and that you do it is to show them that the system is documented, and then have some sort of documentation to show them how the system works in practice. Otherwise they could say, "You say you do this, but where is the evidence to show you do it?". So the system was designed around a documented paper trail to show how you meet the requirements. We bought a standard office manual and tweaked it to meet the requirements of this practice to show we had the standard procedures in place.'

The firm had unwittingly run into trouble in its first inspection by having bought a quality assurance 'package' that no longer reflected what the Legal Services Commission expected from a franchise in having a written policy on age discrimination when recruiting staff:

> 'The template we had used did not say "age" and we'd overlooked the introduction of a requirement where it should say "age", so it was picked up as part of the auditor's checklist. This may seem absurd, but that was one of the requirements. Obviously, the requirement was a firm should have a non-discrimination policy and the policy should make it clear that it will not discriminate against people on the following grounds, race, religion, sex, colour, political affiliation, whatever. It should also have said "age". Ours did not say "age". It was picked up on the audit and we are required to put it right.'

The quality assurance system, however, involved more than having a correctly worded document. It also required the firm to keep documents that enabled auditors to check that there was no discrimination:

'We are also required to keep – and I suppose this is another area of new administrative requirements we did not have previously – you are required to keep copies of everybody's [job applications]. I can't remember if it is everyone who applies for a job or those people who make it on to a shortlist for a job. You also have to keep any notes you make in the interviews with them and I suppose any notes you do as a result of analysing the various CVs when you decided whom you wanted to interview. So not only can the auditor check that our policy says we do not discriminate against people on the grounds of age but he can actually say, "I have seen the notes relating to the recruitment of the last solicitor". He will check to see, well, I suppose, (a) whether we kept them, and (b) if we have kept them, whether we said that we can't recruit him because he's already 60.'

One can begin to see here the amount of work involved in auditing, and also in preparing for audits: in ensuring that the paper trail documents the policy. It is also possible to see the limitations of auditing as a form of 'surveillance': if a candidate had been discriminated against on the grounds of age, but nothing had been noted on the file, this would not affect the quality score achieved by the franchise. The firm could, however, fall down on not having the correct policy, or systems in place (a file containing old job applications) that would in theory allow breaches to be detected.

Another part of the administrative officer's duties was to check that solicitors were keeping their files correctly, according to office procedures, so certain kinds of notes had to be on yellow or red paper to assist the auditors. Solicitors were also required to send letters to clients after each court hearing. This policy had been designed with standard legal aid firms in mind where clients might be represented by different lawyers and not receive proper attention after a hearing. In this firm, solicitors talked to the same client regularly. However, even after spending an afternoon giving legal advice, they were still required to send a letter, so this could be documented on the file:

'It may seem to the client slightly unusual if you've sat next to your client in court on Monday morning for what amounts to an administrative hearing to fix the next date that you have to write to him to confirm that you sat next to him. You speak to him every other day anyway. I think

we know why we have to do it. Sometimes we have to
explain in a letter that we are only doing it because we are
required to do so.'

A major part of the administrator's job was to arrange regular meetings
between solicitors and their supervisors to ensure that office procedures
were being followed, and to document these for a possible inspection.
This was called a 'file review':

Q: What happens in a file review?

A: You have a formal appointment once a month or once every
three months or six months depending on the seniority of the
person involved, and you are required to review a minimum
of two files in the course of that session as a sample against a
checklist designed to reflect the various requirements of what
needs to be on the file, how the file needs to be structured or
what the client needs to be told. They are necessarily things of
a more administrative nature rather than reviewing the quality
of the advice. You have to show the client's been informed of
the name and status of everybody who's working on his case.
He has to be told if people change and the reasons for that. He
has to be given an estimate of the likely costs, and regular costs
information. The file has to reflect that, rather than [the auditor]
looking at the prosecution's case to see if the advice given was
good advice.

It is interesting that quality review in legal services originally started
with checklists (the 'Transaction Criteria') that were intended to allow
auditors to establish if certain quality standards had been met in the
delivery of legal work. Auditors may have had difficulties in practice
in identifying levels of competence from the file. However, the system
now almost entirely focuses on whether administrative procedures,
such as sending letters after court hearings, are being met, and whether
the firm's office manual is correctly worded. This lawyer noted that,
although it benefited clients to keep good records, there was nothing
in the franchising system that ensured that they would receive correct
legal advice:

'At no stage does anyone come in and say that you gave
good advice or that you gave bad advice or that you failed
to advise the client about something in terms of the actual

content of the case. So the requirements and the audit against the requirements are to make sure the practice is run well, that we do tell the clients about costs, but it's not a quality audit in terms of quality of the work.... I suppose you could have the worst lawyers in the world dispensing appalling advice but as long as they complied with the quality mark requirements, no one would ever say you shouldn't be doing this or you should have done it differently.'

Accreditation: a nurse's tale

Although many people, like the manager in this firm of solicitors, take a pragmatic view towards quality assurance, there are others who become frustrated and annoyed. To become really annoyed, completing a form or submitting a quality report has to be experienced as both time-consuming and essentially pointless. Professionals struggling to provide a good quality of service without adequate resources may also have ideological objections. This can be illustrated by considering the case of an Australian nurse who objected to completing the forms required to remain accredited to the local Board of Nursing.

The context that mattered to this interviewee, and which she returned to throughout the interview, was that her workload as a nurse had increased dramatically in the past five years.[9] This is why any new form or procedure was perceived as burdensome: there was not sufficient time to provide a good level of care:

Q: Why has your work increased generally?

A: Because everyone is being discharged from hospital faster. Years ago you would have had half of the ward requiring a lot of care and the other half recuperating and not needing much care at all. So someone who came in for, like, a hysterectomy they would be in for two to three weeks, now they are in for about three [days]. So you've got no one in the ward recuperating. You've got everyone quite ill and as soon as they get a bit better, they're out of the door, they are replaced with someone who is quite ill.

Q: Isn't it a good thing that patients are spending less time in hospital?

A: Well, there is a real assumption they are going to a real home where care will be provided, and for many people that's not true. There's an assumption that if you're looking after children that people will go home and it will not be a financial burden. Both parents have jobs now so it's hard. There's an assumption that they'll get the medication, that they'll be going to an environment that is actually clean and healthy. There's an assumption that parents will have enough knowledge so they can pick up signs and symptoms and that they are perhaps having a relapse.

Q: So, you feel strongly about this?

A: Well, people what we call 'bounce back' a bit more than they used to. You have more admissions coming back in. The other thing is the staffing hasn't increased so if I'm looking after seven patients, 15 years ago three of these patients would have required very little care. Now I've got seven patients requiring more complex care than was available 15 years ago but there's still only me.

Q: Have you come across patients who have gone home too early and something bad has happened to them?

A: Yes, they've just gone home too early and when they come back, they are in a worse condition than we would have picked it up. We would have picked up the early signs.

Q: Is everyone bothered about that?

A: People aren't happy. The morale is very low at the moment where I work and there's not a lot of young people going into nursing and they don't stay.

During the period her workload had increased, there were also more administrative tasks. An example was that the hospital now required nurses to complete admissions and discharge forms for patients. She could see the point of admissions forms, but in the case of discharge no one, as far as she knew, ever looked at these reports. It was like 'sending them off into thin air'. In the case of admissions, there was a requirement to complete a form even if the patient was in long-term care, and so was regularly admitted:

A: Where it does become onerous is where you have patients in long-term care, like being cancer patients, and you do this every time they come in.

Q: You mean you repeat this [procedure] with the same person?

A: Yes, and they are coming in over a two-year period.

Q: Why don't you assume the previous information is correct?

A: Well, because this is part of the process. We have a process and we're going to go through it.

Q: Right. But is this maybe a safety net to check if someone has moved?

A: Well, they may have moved but mostly they don't. If [someone] has cancer, they won't move in the beginning. The pre-existing condition is not going to change.

Q: So when you explain it to them, you've got to do this form again, how do they respond?

A: We both roll our eyes and we just, you know, I go through it really quickly.

These procedures were accepted as part of everyday work. However, there were other administrative tasks that she experienced as not simply irritating, but burdensome. One was the periodic inspection of the hospital, during which staff had to learn administrative procedures by rote, such as the emergency codes for announcements over the public address system. In the case of an unusual emergency, one could easily 'lift and look' since the codes were attached to a nurse's uniform, but for the purposes of inspection you were required 'to spit them out of your head'.

The quality assurance procedures this nurse most resented were the annual performance review interview, which she had avoided for the past three years without anyone following it up, and the five-year audit conducted by the Nursing Board. The work involved was considerable in that nurses had to supply examples of practice and write them up to illustrate a number of key competences:

'There's one on interpersonal skills and there's basic nursing practice like infection control. You can do anything and link it. They are quite broad. Leadership is one of them and you can talk about having run a shift. Education another. You are constantly educating people either patients or their parents or other nurses.'

Completing the report was not straightforward:

'The appraisal form is quite complicated. The way you have to write it out is to write it to a formula. You have to link what you did to the competences, so it is a fiddly process.'

The auditee also had to provide reading lists to demonstrate that, in the previous five years, she had been keeping up with professional reading. There was, however, no time to keep records on a busy ward, and nowhere to keep the records:

'It's really difficult since my work's not organised. You have a desk, so if you want to jot something down you can if you chose to. I don't have a desk. I have no space in my work environment to even keep a list.'

These are complaints about the work involved in completing the report, which would probably mean staying late or working at home. It is also evident that this interviewee did not like being assessed (hospital inspections created 'a real fear'), and resented the fact she was being asked to demonstrate competence, despite being locally accountable to her own managers and a professional workgroup.

Ticking the boxes

The experiences reported in these case studies do not suggest that professionals are overwhelmed or that their work is made impossible by quality assurance. They do not report having reached breaking point because of the amount of time spent filling in forms and writing quality reports, or from anxiety over inspections. They may dislike the regulation, and find it 'ridiculous', but most take the pragmatic view that it is easier to work within the system than to ask difficult questions or campaign against agencies such as the Legal Services Commission or National Health and Medical Research Council.[10] Those in management positions also find that, with sufficient thought and planning, it is usually possible to obtain a good score, since what is being assessed is not the quality of work performed by professional staff, but whether or not the organisation is well managed. In practice, this means that they have to demonstrate compliance with the idealised model for setting and reviewing goals, and identifying problems recommended in business tools such as the Excellence Model for achieving continuous improvement.

One informal managerial practice that has developed inside the public sector for satisfying quality inspections is known as 'ticking the boxes'. The following account by a former head of department in a 'new' university illustrates how this works as a pragmatic response to quality assurance:

> 'I am glad I don't have to do that job anymore. You just have to learn how to tick the boxes. You have to show the next year that you have done what you said you would do, and someone has the job of checking this, so they have a paper or audit trail. The only way to survive this is to say what you have already done, or know what is going to happen. To give an example, if you know there will be a change in the way a course is taught, you write this up as having identified a problem, and that you will be deciding on action to remedy this. The decision has already been made, and the action may already have been taken – but it appears that it will be happening in the next year. Then you can tick the boxes and everyone is happy. You would be creating problems for yourself if you did not do this.'

In fact, the system has become so elaborate in some universities that similar procedures are employed by lecturers when providing an annual report about their own teaching:

> 'You do not have to say that you are making changes every year, but you need to say you are making changes some years, otherwise someone might ask you about this. I sometimes do not fill in this section – I have become cynical about it.'

This procedure for making it appear that objectives are achieved each year is, however, never completely risk-free:

> 'The annoying thing is that if you do this properly, the real
> problems that can happen are never reported on the forms,
> or only appear the following year. You just have to show
> that you are making some changes. You also have to be
> careful that you are not caught out – that something does
> not appear on minutes out of the blue.'

Although it is difficult to measure, a great deal of unseen work is
required by professionals to make quality assurance work as a system
of regulation. To put this differently, the elaborate tables used to set
objectives and review success in achieving these, which have become
so much a part of organisational life in the past 20 years, do not reflect
what actually happens inside organisations. Nevertheless, the activities
of any work group have to be presented, year on year, as achieving
continuous improvement within this framework.

A negative case study

To present a balanced picture, it seems important to make it clear that
there are many professionals who do not find quality assurance
initiatives burdensome, who simply accept this form of regulation as a
routine part of their ordinary working lives.[11] This can be illustrated
by an interview with a general practitioner in Australia. Medical
professionals here have fewer complaints about quality assurance
initiatives (which are more developed in the United Kingdom) but
there are other types of paperwork and administrative procedures that
doctors are required to undertake as part of their obligations to other
government agencies.

   Professional associations representing general practitioners have
complained about growing levels of paperwork for many years, in
addition to the burdens involved in obtaining and maintaining
accreditation. These include the work involved in completing
Centrelink forms to enable patients to claim disability and other
benefits, or obtaining permission to prescribe certain types of drugs.
Submissions to a report by the Productivity Commission included
the following complaint about the stress and frustration involved in
completing forms:

> The administrative burden of "paperwork requirement" is
> a source of complaint, the time it takes to meet these
> requirements is now beginning to seriously "eat into" time
> which should be spent on patient care and consultations. If

paperwork requirements are not met during normal consulting hours, these matters have to be attended to out of consulting hours, which contributes to "burn out", ill-health and stress related issues. (Productivity Commission, 2003, p 70)

By contrast, the practitioner interviewed for this study did not see managing the work of completing forms, as well as seeing patients, as particularly burdensome:

'No, personally I don't find the paperwork too much. Sometimes things can come up in the day that take up time. So yesterday, I should have finished at half past twelve but I left at quarter past two. But that was related to someone who is unwell, and I had to pull out a result and talk to a specialist, and he told me what we needed to do next, which involved organising another specialist and then having to ring the patient back to tell her. That's not so much paperwork but it's still work around all that. That all takes time. Then I would document all that: that I've spoken to him, that I've spoken to her, and the patient knows what's happening, this is what the plan is. These are probably the things that take more time – having to ring people.'

This interviewee also did not have much sympathy for those who complained about stress:

'I think it depends on the person. There are a lot of people who are really well organised. I think that the people who seem to run late, start late. They might turn up on time but they don't actually start seeing their patients until mid-morning, so their day is really extended. I'm not really like that [laughs]. Then there are people who worry a lot, and spend a lot of time probably at work reading or looking things up on the internet, because they worry a lot about patients. And everyone's different, like in any job, in the amount they take home with them.... Perhaps for me it has become normal work. I was told by the first people I worked with that you have half an hour at the end [after seeing patients] to do your bits and pieces. I find that the normal way you do things, whereas other people might find that restrictive.'

One interesting feature of this interview with a newly qualified doctor is that features of traditional professionalism, such as worrying a lot about patients and keeping up with new techniques, are seen as undesirable qualities if they prevent you finishing appointments with sufficient time to complete the paperwork. Learning organisational skills, including the ability to start on time, are as important in medical practice as having good listening and communication skills or knowledge of medicine. Another interesting feature is that the burden from red tape, or quality assurance as a form of red tape, is experienced differently depending on the type of work done, or the level of administrative responsibility. The interviewee knew that those doing work for nursing homes had a lot of additional paperwork, and that anyone managing a practice had to contend with preparing for accreditation inspections. This was partly why general practices in Australia and elsewhere are encountering problems in persuading younger professionals to take on management responsibilities.

Finally, it is worth noting that, even though she did not view red tape as a problem, this general practitioner identified one new procedure that created unnecessary administrative work. This was a requirement by the hospital that the doctor supply a letter requesting a referral to a particular consultant in a diabetes clinic, since it needed this to claim funding back from the Commonwealth government:

A: It seems like for me, from my perspective, to be a little bit a waste of time, because if I am sending someone to a diabetes clinic you don't know which doctor you're going to get, but now the patient is ringing back and saying, 'Now I've been told by the hospital you need to write a letter to Dr. Smith', and then you have to do it again.

Q Why didn't you do this the first time?

A: Because you might not know they needed to see Dr. Smith. If you fill it in to see Dr. Smith, they might say he's on leave or not back for another six months so you have to see Dr. Jones now, so I've found lately that sort of duplicates things and is annoying. That annoys me [laughs]. It is something else we have to do and makes it confusing for the patient. They worry that they're not going to be able to see anybody. I think that a lot of patients entering the public system are aware they don't have a lot of control over who they are going to see, but that is something that seems to have just happened, which I find is annoying because there seems to be no set guideline. They could just say, 'Refer to someone, and if that's not possible we will just change the name ourselves'.

This is a good example of red tape, in that it proved impossible to make an appointment without sending two letters. It also created work in that the doctor had to reassure the patient. The work involved was not particularly burdensome, but for this professional it was experienced as 'annoying' because it seemed unnecessary.

Government initiatives to reduce red tape

One conclusion that might be drawn from these case studies is that red tape is a significant social problem that is not taken sufficiently seriously by politicians. After all, it would appear that quality assurance initiatives, along with other demands on professionals to supply information to outside agencies, take up a great deal of time that could be spent in delivering services. At its worst, red tape can cause sickness or stress in overworked public employees, and lead to doctors, teachers, police officers and university lecturers leaving these occupations. One might conclude that the growing amount of regulation created by the massive expansion of government in the last century itself requires some form of supervision and regulation.

Regulating the regulators

Although they have a low public profile, there are in fact government agencies that have exactly this role: to monitor regulatory agencies and ensure they do not burden the public, business or public sector professionals with excessive bureaucracy. The first country to recognise red tape as a problem was the United States, which established the Office of Information and Regulatory Affairs (OIRA) inside the Office of Management and Budget, the Executive Office of the President, through the 1995 Paperwork Reduction Act (PRA). This piece of legislation set 'government wide burden hour reduction goals of 10% for the fiscal year (FY) 1996 and FY 1997, and 5% for FY 1998 – FY 2001' (US Department of Labor, 2002). OIRA reports annually to a congressional committee, and publishes lists of agencies that have complied with their statutory requirements under PRA.

In Britain, the Regulatory Impact Unit and Better Regulation Task Force, based in the Cabinet Office, have a similar role in reducing bureaucracy and red tape. The Task Force was established by Tony

Blair in 1999, two years after coming to power, with a mission to improve the quality of regulation. It has produced several reports making recommendations to reduce paperwork in different areas of government (for example, Better Regulation Task Force, 2005). In Australia, the Productivity Commission, which collects performance information about government departments, has also started initiatives to combat red tape (for example, Productivity Commission, 2003). The chair, Gary Banks (2003), noted in a talk given to a business symposium that 'the burgeoning of regulation and its increasing complexity are major irritants for the regulated'. Some states of Australia have also established their own agencies to reduce red tape. In Queensland, the Red Tape Reduction Task Force provides advice and assistance to agencies to help them comply with the Regulatory Impact Statement process set up by the 1992 Statutory Instruments Act. This requires any department considering new legislation to prepare a statement reviewing the costs and benefits of different regulatory options.

These agencies have not been content with documenting complaints, but have also attempted to quantify the burden by asking those affected to provide estimates of the time taken in completing different forms. This has been taken furthest in America, where OIRA has calculated the actual burden hours in particular years, making it possible to provide a target of the number of hours that need to be reduced to meet the PRA targets. Its annual reports provide an interesting commentary both on the amount of apparently unnecessary paper generated by modern organisations and the scientific confidence informing attempts to measure and reduce this in a search for continuous improvement. One report contains a table showing how 'actual burden hours' fell from 241,039,796 during the 1996 fiscal year to 186,108,821 in 2001. It also achieved 'burden hour reduction goals' in 1996 and 1997 of 10%, and the burden was further reduced by 4% in 1998, 2% in 1999, 7% in 2000 and 2% in 2001 (US Department of Labour, 2002).

This report makes clear that it would be difficult to remove red tape entirely (to reduce the burden hours to zero). In 2002, there was an ambitious target of reducing the burden by 29%. If this were achieved, the Paperwork Reduction Act would have reduced the paperwork burden on the American government by almost half in its first six years: a considerable achievement, but one that raises questions about how the burden is measured and whether people and organisations on the ground feel any happier about bureaucracy.

The Regulatory Impact Unit

To obtain a clearer picture of what is involved in measuring and reducing red tape, this section focuses on the work of the Regulatory Impact Unit in Britain. This is based in the Cabinet Office, a government agency reporting directly to the Prime Minister, and shares offices with the Better Regulation Task Force. In 2003, it consisted of seven people, two of whom were permanent civil servants and the rest seconded from industry. A representative interviewed had a background in process management from working in the gas industry, and believed that the same techniques could be used to reduce paperwork in the public sector.

The unit does not systematically monitor government agencies, in the same way as its American counterpart, but produces reports at the request of ministers or other interested parties. A good example of the approach can be found in a report about red tape in general practice. A flavour of the optimistic character of the language used by New Labour in its second term in office can be found in the preface by Tony Blair:

> Last year, I put forward 10 key ideas that would reduce the bureaucratic burden on GPs, better utilise the skills of other health professionals, and increase the amount of time that family doctors could spend with those who need their expertise most. These ideas were enshrined in the NHS plan that the Government published last July, but we were also determined to take action that would have a more immediate effect.

> The report sets out the interim outcomes of an ongoing project by the Cabinet Office Public Sector Team to reduce GP red tape and bureaucracy. It follows similar work by the Team to reduce burdens on police and head teachers. The report describes action that has been taken in six out of the 10 areas I identified last year. At first glance the individual outcomes may in themselves appear minor and inconsequential. But a key message from this exercise is that when a number of minor changes are added together, they make a real difference to the overall burden on front-line service providers in the public sector, in this case GPs. This is a lesson we should all take to heart – however small a request we feel a request to be, however little time we

believe it would take to complete it, we need to remember that it is probably just one among many. We want our GPs to be treating patients and improving health generally – their time is too precious to be wasted on other activities. (Regulatory Impact Unit, 2001, p 1).

To achieve this objective, the Regulatory Impact Unit started by establishing an advisory group. The team consulted a group of 25 GPs and obtained submissions from 33 stakeholder organisations. It also visited GP surgeries 'to hear at first hand how red tape and bureaucracy can get in the way of treating patients' (Regulatory Impact Unit, 2001, p 10). From this it compiled a list of '65 areas for attention', and then focused on 29 of these, with the aim of identifying changes that 'would make a real difference'. As one usually finds in government reports of this kind, no interviews are presented that illustrate how GPs felt about red tape, or their response to being visited by civil servants concerned about this issue. Instead, estimates are provided of the time taken in dealing with particular forms. The unit then approached the department responsible, and in many cases were successful in removing what it calls 'unnecessary GP input'.

To give an example, GPs complained about the work involved in countersigning passport applications. The unit approached the Passport Office and asked it to remove 'reference to doctors as counter-signatories' in the new version of its guidance notes and forms. This is estimated to make an annual saving of 217,000 appointments plus 54,000 hours (presumably where patients supply forms for signature by a doctor without requiring an appointment). In total, the first report on reducing GP paperwork claimed to have achieved an annual saving of 7.2 million appointments and 750,000 hours. A follow-up report, based on a questionnaire 'completed by 36 GPs', claimed that this resulted in 'potential savings' of 3.2 million appointments, 2.7 million hours: a saving equivalent to 'the number of appointments conducted by 1,200 typical GPs in a working year'.

The politics of red tape

Having described different dimensions of red tape as a social or organisational phenomenon, it seems worth reconsidering Gouldner's (1952) constructionist perspective. It should be remembered that Gouldner did not see red tape as entirely in the eye of the beholder: it had an objective component in terms of how bureaucracies actually behaved (so there could be real examples of poorly designed forms and unnecessary procedures) as well as a subjective element in that people responded differently to this treatment.

There seems to be no evidence to support Gouldner's belief that bureaucratic regulation most irritates and frustrates people with conservative views, at least in our own times when everyone accepts the need for a large public sector. However, it is clear that views differ about bureaucracy. The agencies carrying out inspections and creating new regulations must believe that the benefits outweigh the costs. On the other hand, many professionals and managers in schools, hospitals, doctors' surgeries, police forces and universities complain about excessive regulation. People experience this differently, or have different ways of coping, and some do not recognise paperwork or regulation as burdensome. Nevertheless, government reports accept that red tape is a real problem, and genuine efforts are being made to reduce unnecessary regulation.

If red tape is a subjective issue, then its existence will depend on the ability of groups and individuals to have their concerns recognised (Mauss, 1975; Best, 1995). Government units concerned with reducing red tape were established primarily because of pressure exerted on politicians from powerful groups such as the General Medical Council and Association of Head Teachers. This is not to suggest that there is something tokenistic or hypocritical about efforts by government to reduce the red tape it creates through its own activities. However, it is hard to challenge powerful regulatory agencies. An example of this can be found in a passage in a Better Regulation Task Force report (2002) on burdens in higher education commenting on the RAE. The Task Force had received submissions that not only was it expensive and bureaucratic (according to one estimate, the cost of the 1996 RAE was 'in the region of £35m'), but it was also arbitrary and unfair to those participating. A major cause for complaint was that the 'goalposts' had been moved when it was announced that in the 2001 RAE those achieving lower grades would no longer receive funding, even though they had made a substantial financial contribution to participate. The Task Force accepted these criticisms, but could only congratulate the Higher Education Funding Council (HEFC) on announcing an internal review of its own procedures:

> We welcome HEFC's commitment to a wide-ranging review of the RAE. It has acknowledged there are widespread concerns about its impact particularly in terms of the funding implications and effects on individuals and institutions....We would expect any replacement or revised

RAE to meet the Principles of Good Regulation. (Better
Regulation Task Force, 2002, p 22)

This is similar to the approach taken by government agencies concerned
with regulating red tape. Most readily admit that they have no real
power to change other agencies or stop them regulating. The most
that can be done is require them to review the costs and benefits of
legislation through a 'Regulatory Impact Statement'. Ironically, of
course, regulatory agencies like the Better Regulation Task Force can
themselves generate red tape, by requiring other agencies to publish
self-assessments 'for consultation', and requesting public service
professionals complete more forms on how they spend their time.
Additionally, one gets the impression that as one tentacle of the octopus
of red tape is removed (usually through some group putting political
pressure on government), another grows elsewhere through some other
regulatory or legislative programme. Despite the charts and tables
produced, continuous improvement in reducing red tape may be as
difficult to achieve as improvements in other areas of government.

Notes

[1] According to Gouldner (1952), the term originated in early 19th-
century England. Thomas Carlyle, for example, described a political
opponent as 'little other than a red-tape talking machine'. The
sociologist Herbert Spencer used the term in 1873 to describe
bureaucracy.

[2] Opponents of bureaucracy during the 1970s included right-wingers
influenced by Hayek (1979) who believed that the welfare state
inhibited enterprise and self-reliance but also left-wingers seeking to
expose the failings and 'contradictions' of the state in addressing social
problems (for example, Habermas, 1973).

[3] Goodsell (1983, p 22) makes much of the fact that two thirds of
respondents in a Harris poll rated the federal, state and local government
in America as 'helpful' or 'very helpful'. Critics of bureaucracy would,
of course, be more interested in the fact that one third reported their
experiences with government as 'unhelpful'. Interestingly, towards the
end of his study, Goodsell proposes an information campaign to make
people appreciate bureaucracy, through having more realistic
expectations.

[4] Unfortunately, Gouldner does not give any information about how the interviewees were selected. Particular interviews are not analysed in depth, and there is no analysis of negative cases where interviewees did not experience administrative procedures as bureaucratic.

[5] The complaint seems to be not against the fact that we depend on professionals or experts in modern societies, but that professionals in large organisations treat people impersonally through following bureaucratic rules.

[6] This area of regulation started in America during the early 1970s, and was established in Canada and Australia during the 1990s through primary legislation. It was introduced into Britain in 2005 by the Economic and Social Research Council, which funds university research.

[7] It takes time learning how to prepare ethics applications, but those who succeed can become part of the regulatory system as consultants. This is how regulatory systems create a network of people with a financial or emotional stake in the system that can develop into a professional mission.

[8] Critics have complained that people interviewed on sensitive topics are unwilling to sign consent forms, so this requirement makes it difficult or impossible to conduct empirical research. Particular difficulties arise in interviewing young people about their sexual behaviour or criminal activities in that ethics committees, at least in Australia, require researchers to obtain written consent from parents.

[9] For a Canadian qualitative study that documents these changes in some detail, see Rankin and Campbell (2006).

[10] It is, in fact, quite difficult to object to this kind of regulation, other than through participating in consultation exercises, which assume that everyone believes that quality assurance is valuable and necessary. My experience of dealing with ethics committees is that political statements made on applications are simply ignored: all the regulatory body cares about is compliance through, for example, submitting a consent form that is correctly worded.

[11] Qualitative traditions concerned with scientific accuracy often recommend looking for negative cases, since these allow one to deepen the analysis (see, for example, Strauss and Corbin, 1998).

SEVEN

Critical responses

Two recent critics
- Power on auditing
- O'Neill on trust

Marxism and quality assurance
- The deskilling debate
- Proletarianisation and professionals
- Neo-liberalism and public services

Foucault and governmentality
- Foucault's criticisms of Marxism
- The governmentality tradition
- A Foucauldian view of quality assurance

Habermas and Luhmann on regulation
- The colonisation of the lifeworld
- The limits of law

How persuasive are the critics?
- A question of values
- The problem of the professions

Chapter Six gave a taste of the outright hostility towards quality assurance expressed by some public sector professionals. Although this is by no means shared by everyone working in schools, hospitals, universities and police forces, one does not need to conduct a survey to know that these initiatives are not universally liked, and cause at the very least irritation among those who have to prepare for inspections or write up internal quality reports. This, however, raises the question of whether anyone has expressed these objections more systematically or in a way that might persuade senior civil servants and politicians to question the value of quality assurance. This chapter looks at the intellectual criticisms raised by academics who have written about this issue from a variety of theoretical perspectives.

The chapter starts by looking at the recent critiques published in the United Kingdom by Michael Power (1997) and Onora O'Neill (2002), which have received a reasonable level of attention in the media through arguing that quality assurance is ritualistic and damages trust in professionals. It then looks at some critical traditions in sociology and draws out ideas and arguments that are relevant to quality assurance. It considers the Marxist field of labour process studies that was influential during the 1970s and 1980s, and the Foucauldian governmentality tradition that has, arguably, replaced Marxism as the natural vehicle for critical politics. It also considers the wider argument made by the critical systems theorist Jürgen Habermas (1973, 1987) during the 1970s on the problems created by over-regulation in the modern world, and similar ideas developed by Niklas Luhmann (1985, 1995) on the limits of law. Finally, it considers the persuasiveness of the criticisms, and the extent to which they escape the difficulty of appearing to defend the traditional privileges of professionals.

Two recent critics

Although there are large literatures in political science, public administration and management studies about managerialism, the new public management and neo-liberalism, only a few studies have examined quality assurance as a new form of regulation in any degree of depth. These include Pollitt's (1993) investigation of the political implications and effects of the new public management particularly on the British National Health Service, David Marquand's (2004) critique of public sector reforms, some of the theoretical pieces in Marilyn Strathern's (2000) collection considering the effects of auditing and inspection on higher education, Ian Kirkpatrick and Miguel Martinez Lucio's (1995) collection about the introduction of quality management across the public sector, and Paul du Gay's (2000) writings on management and bureaucracy.[1]

   Although all these studies have some political content, and are critical towards quality assurance, they have been written for academic audiences and have not made much impact outside universities. There are, however, two studies that have reached a wider audience, and could be described as contributions to 'public sociology' (Agger, 2000; Burawoy, 2005). These are Michael Power's (1997) *The audit society* and Onora O'Neill's (2002) *A question of trust*. Power's argument was originally published as a pamphlet by Demos, a left-wing think tank, in a series concerned with renewal and change in the United Kingdom (Power, 1994). O'Neill's book was delivered as the 2002 Reith Lectures and received widespread praise from politicians and journalists. They remain the fullest and most thoughtful critiques of quality assurance that have so far been advanced, even though they have had no impact whatsoever on British public policy.

Power on auditing

Michael Power was originally an accountant, before becoming a professor of accounting at the London School of Economics and Political Science, and the central argument in his book, *The audit society*, is that auditing has spread from the financial sphere to public administration, with damaging consequences for the organisations that deliver public services, and for society in general. He is critical towards financial auditing for not protecting society against fraud or mismanagement, and believes that the same problems arise when it is used to assure quality in the public services.

Financial audits have formed part of the world of commerce and industry for many years, and a central task of the accountancy profession has been to audit company accounts to check that the figures in the annual reports reflect actual performance (see Harper, 1989). This involves visiting the head offices of companies and examining a sample of accounting records to ensure that figures are being entered correctly, and the proper systems are in place. At the time Power was writing, a series of financial scandals demonstrated that auditors could look the other way, even when there was no suggestion of underhand dealings, and that it is relatively easy for companies to conceal damaging information from auditors and shareholders. However, in his view, the really strange feature of auditing is that there is no reliable or scientific procedure available to tell whether a company is doing well or badly:

> Not only is it unclear what auditing is for but, even if this could be agreed, it would still be very unclear how well auditing serves the purposes for which it was intended and whether, in particular circumstances, it really succeeds or fails. There is no robust conception of 'good' auditing independent either of auditor judgements or of the system of knowledge in which those judgements are embedded and against which particular audits can be judged. Good auditing ends up as conformity to agreed procedures which have stood the test of time. (Power, 1997, p 29)

Another way of putting this is that financial auditing involves exercising judgement, rather than being a science. Auditors themselves can differ on whether to give a company a clean bill of health for its internal accounting procedures; similarly, those concerned with the performance of companies can question the results of an audit. Power notes that 'as a result the success or failure of auditing is never a public fact but is always an object of persistent dispute, an adversarial process in which questions of blame are at stake' (Power, 1997, p 29). This suggests that all financial audits can do is provide reassurance that everything is in order, without protecting companies from fraud or scandals, or even allowing investors to make well-informed decisions.

Auditing has been extended beyond looking at financial records, and firms of accountants are employed in the public sector to conduct 'value for money' and performance auditing. Performance auditing has been conducted for governments since the 1980s through organisations such as the General Accounting Office in America and the Audit Commission in the United Kingdom. They conduct evaluative studies, based on analysing documents and interviewing management teams in a similar way to consultants in the private sector. However, the British government went even further by establishing a programme of Best Value audits on all local authorities. More generally, the models and procedures used originally in financial auditing were gradually taken up by government inspectorates in how they assessed public sector managers. Organisations such as schools, hospitals and police forces were now expected to have internal audit systems in place. The task of an external auditor or inspector was to check these systems in a similar way to how financial auditors check that a company keeps proper records.

It will come as no surprise that Power believes that performance auditing is just as unreliable as financial auditing in identifying poor performance. Here he draws on a literature by American political scientists about the unintended consequences of government regulation (Power, 1997, pp 95-6). Meyer and Rowan (1991) had already argued, in an influential article, that regulation could become 'decoupled' from the work of providing services on the ground. This suggests that a whole tier of management can arise that collects information of little relevance to actual performance:

> From this point of view, audits are 'rationalized rituals of inspection' which produce comfort, and hence organizational legitimacy, by attending to formal control structures and auditible performance measures. Even though audit files are created, checklists get completed and performance is measured and monitored in ever more elaborate detail, audit concerns itself with auditable form rather than substance. (Power, 1997, p 96)

A more damaging possibility is that auditing affects how practitioners make decisions, so that it becomes what Sieber (1981) calls a 'fatal remedy'. This means that practitioners do not simply tolerate auditing, but are shaped and influenced by the auditing process ('colonisation'). In Power's words, this can lead to 'the creation over time of new mentalities, new incentives and perceptions of significance' (Power, 1997, p 97). One example he gives is the Research Assessment Exercise (RAE) in which researchers have been told, at various times, that panels will give no credit for writing textbooks and that refereed articles in 'top' journals are more valuable than monographs. The RAE has not, therefore, simply created new administrative tasks inside universities, but has changed the nature of academic work.

Power places more emphasis in his book on the problem of 'decoupling' as against 'colonisation', although to some extent they are connected since the work involved in reporting can distract practitioners from their core tasks. He concludes that rather than solving problems of performance, audit 'emerges more as a new form of image management' (Power, 1997, p 143). Without directly saying that it should be reduced or abolished, he suggests that the problem lies in assuming that a standardised approach for regulation will work, whereas 'regulatory sensitivity about what makes organisations like schools and hospitals effective is necessary'. The sensitive regulator would make decisions 'about how to leave individuals alone to get on with their work as much as about how to monitor them' (Power, 1997, p 145). Although the book is written in academic language, Power is, therefore, highly critical towards auditing, and to some extent can be seen as making similar objections to professionals who have spoken out against excessive regulation. He argues that it is ritualistic, rather than having any real economic or social value, and raises expectations that cannot be delivered.

O'Neill on trust

In her (2002) Reith Lectures, the Cambridge philosopher Onora O'Neill also argued that excessive regulation can actually damage performance by interfering in professional judgement:

> Even those who devise the indicators know that they are at very best surrogates for the real objectives. Nobody after all seriously thinks that the number of exam passes are the only evidence of good teaching, or that crime clear-up rates are the only evidence of good policing. Some exams

> are easier, others are harder; some crimes are easier to clear up, others are harder. However, the performance indicators have a deep effect on professional and institutional behaviour. If a certain 'A'-level board offers easier examinations in a subject, schools have reason to choose that syllabus *even if it is educationally inferior*. If waiting lists can be reduced faster by concentrating on certain medical procedures, hospitals have every reason so to do, even if medical priorities differ. Perverse incentives are real incentives. I think we all know that from our daily lives. (O'Neill, 2002, p 55; emphasis in original)

O'Neill goes further than Powell in suggesting that trust, both in established institutions and professional expertise, is necessary for society. By and large, the ordinary person does trust people like scientists, doctors and even journalists and politicians. When polled by journalists or social scientists, they often express dissatisfaction, but not to the extent of seeking alternatives. Even so, O'Neill argues that the mistakes made by professionals, and the problems that have always existed in complex organisations, have been exaggerated. In her view, there is no evidence for a 'crisis of trust', but 'we have massive evidence of a culture of suspicion' (O'Neill, 2002, p 18).

Although it is not entirely clear from the lectures how this is generated, two possibilities are worth considering. The first, which draws on Durkheim's writings on the modern world, is that the reverse side of trust is always fear and anxiety. This is why Durkheim believed that even the most orderly society would suffer from regular moral panics. These could be managed by good government but not eliminated. He also argued that they had symbolic value in reaffirming shared values and objectives. From this perspective, no one can be blamed for excessive or harmful regulation and, in any event, the harm can be exaggerated. The second possibility, which is concerned with the mechanisms in generating fear and mistrust, is that particular groups are engaged in promoting the need for quality assurance. These benefit from anxiety to the extent that this creates more work for regulators. One can find this argument made in relation to the making of criminal laws against 'deviant' groups in the interactionist labelling tradition (Becker, 1963). Although Power and O'Neill do not refer to these sociological literatures, one reading of their work is that they see the rapid rise of quality assurance as a moral panic. Like Durkheim, they are not opposed to law and the state, or liberal democracy as a form of government, but see excessive regulation as potentially harmful.

Marxism and quality assurance

The best way of appreciating what is distinctive and valuable about the work of Power and O'Neill, and to understand its limitations, is to consider the arguments of sociologists who have advanced a more radical, leftist critique of contemporary society. During the 1970s, the most influential tradition in Britain was Marxism, which focused on the economic inequalities produced by a capitalist society. One variety of Marxism that flourished during this period was the tradition of labour process studies founded by Harry Braverman (1974). Although few sociologists these days would describe themselves as Marxists, at least without considerable qualification, this remains influential in understanding technological and other changes in the workplace.[2] Those influenced by this tradition are ultimately interested in the distribution of income and wealth in society, and how this is changing, so their analysis is quite distinct from that advanced by Power and O'Neill.

The deskilling debate

Marx is mostly remembered today as a failed prophet, given that the economic polarisation he predicted between property owners and the unemployed masses who will form a revolutionary political movement has not so far happened. The prediction that workers' wages would fall, and they would experience long periods of unemployment or underemployment as work was mechanised, was based on his observations of the effect of booms and slumps on the cotton industry during the British industrial revolution (Marx and Engels, 1979). However, Marx also believed that the effective exploitation of labour in factories meant that work would become increasingly unsatisfying, even while wages remained high. There would also be an unhealthy polarisation between those doing unsatisfying manual jobs and an elite of intellectuals who would manage the production process. The experience of unfulfilling work, and the loss of control to managers, would itself create industrial unrest, which in the right conditions would become directed against the whole capitalist system.

Braverman (1974) sought to demonstrate that this process of deskilling continued in the 20th century. It was central to Taylor's (1990) conception of scientific management that involved breaking down tasks into smaller units, and employing managers and technical experts to study the labour process. Technological development, including mechanisation, had also created casualised, low-paid workers who could easily be replaced at the bottom of organisational hierarchies. Braverman argued that this had already happened in factories, with the automated production line. It had also changed the nature of office work, and by the mid-1970s it was apparent that computerisation would not only create mass unemployment but also reduce the skills required in clerical jobs.

There is a large academic literature that sought to test Braverman's thesis of proletarianisation and deskilling during the 1970s and 1980s (for example, Thompson, 1983). Many commentators came to the view that empirical research did not support the main argument. In manufacturing industry there are, for example, industries where teams of workers exercise higher levels of skill and autonomy producing just-in-time products using new technology for high wages. Claims that computerisation would result in mass unemployment and the 'end of work' have also been proved wrong. Some manufacturing and clerical jobs have disappeared, but new jobs have been created, especially in the service sector. There has also been an expansion of professional, managerial and administrative jobs, including those associated with quality assurance.

In response to these criticisms, supporters of Braverman have argued that many workers have been deskilled, so there is a difference between working in a call centre or fast-food restaurant to the manufacturing industries that disappeared in Britain during the 1980s. They also shifted ground, arguing that the key issue had never been solely the level of skill used in a job, but also the extent to which workers enjoyed job security and freedom from close supervision. Employment in a capitalist enterprise may involve being given responsibility over work, or being taught new skills, but the worker still has no control over the product, and is vulnerable during an economic downturn, or if production is moved overseas to countries with cheaper labour costs.

Proletarianisation and professionals

Marxist writers have argued that Braverman's predictions about deskilling are equally relevant to the work of public sector professionals (Sinclair et al, 1996; Harris, 1998). To simplify a complex set of arguments, it has been suggested that although the state is to some extent isolated from market pressures, there are economic pressures for it to exploit labour more effectively in order to reduce or at least control public spending. This means that governments in recent times have attempted to keep down wages and improve productivity through closer supervision and direction of workers, reorganising the labour process, and investing in new technology. To determine whether this argument is correct requires answering the following questions:

- Have skill levels deteriorated among teachers, doctors, lawyers or university lecturers employed in public sector organisations?
- Do managers supervise and direct work more closely?
- Have economic rewards and employment conditions deteriorated across the public sector?
- Has this led to discontent and industrial unrest?

There are no simple answers, just as there is no way of verifying Braverman's claims about the labour process in manufacturing, clerical work or the service industries. One can find examples that support a particular side of the argument, but there are usually also counter-examples, so in the end empirical research is only persuasive if one accepts or is sympathetic towards Marx's long-term predictions for capitalism. There is also the problem that some professional occupations are better placed to resist managerial reforms than others: the older professions, particularly doctors and lawyers, have been more successful than teachers or social workers in retaining control of their work, and maintaining levels of pay, although there are also considerable differences within particular professions. Although there is evidence that workloads in different occupations have increased (for example, Easthope and Easthope, 2000; Harrison and Dowswell 2002), and professionals are subject to greater managerial supervision and control, it is easy to exaggerate the extent of the changes.

Notwithstanding these criticisms, it should be apparent that labour process theory provides a significantly different way of understanding the rise of quality assurance to Power and O'Neill. One could even argue from this perspective that when professionals complain about quality assurance as a ritualistic activity, they are really concerned about the deterioration of their working conditions and loss of autonomy. Against this, one might add that public sector professionals, like workers in the private sector, have not demonstrated great industrial militancy in recent years.

Neo-liberalism and public services

Because their economic policies create greater economic inequality, neo-liberal governments also favour, or face pressures to create, a two-tier system of healthcare, schooling and higher education. There has, of course, always been a two-tier system in the developed world, even though social democratic governments tried to reduce this by redistributing property and wealth through taxation, and establishing institutions concerned with providing services on the basis of need such as the National Health Service. Neo-liberal governments have not so far radically reformed these institutions, but they welcome the fact that those who work hard, and so earn higher incomes, should be able to benefit by purchasing better services. In hospitals, this has meant introducing a market into health services, so those with higher incomes can obtain a better quality of service. In higher education, it has meant concentrating resources to support research in elite institutions, without making significant progress in increasing access to higher education for those from lower-income backgrounds. It is hard to separate quality assurance initiatives from these developments, since they are often used as tools to achieve restructuring.

One can, therefore, argue that when doctors or lecturers complain about quality assurance, they are really concerned about the effects of neo-liberal economic and social policies. There is, however, no evidence that most professionals, or for that matter workers in manufacturing industry, see their problems at work in terms of this larger picture. One weakness of the Marxist tradition, which partly explains why the rich body of theoretical and empirical work about alienation and deskilling published during the 1970s and 1980s ultimately led nowhere, is that many workers and professionals enjoy their work, and do not see their relationship with managers in class terms.

Foucault and governmentality

Another critical theorist who has developed a considerable following across a number of academic disciplines since the 1980s is Michel Foucault, whose ideas originally developed as a critique of the French Communist Party for its rigid belief in class struggle as the motor of history. Foucault has, among other things, inspired a body of theorising and research in political science and sociology known as the 'governmentality' tradition (Burchell et al, 1991; Rose and Miller, 1992; Rose, 1996; Dean, 1999). In its pure and conceptually developed form, this has arguably less political content than Marxist studies of the labour process, although it has been adopted by many sociologists as a vehicle for siding with marginal or disadvantaged groups, or writing critically about social issues.[3] Because there are a variety of approaches within the tradition, and it can be used in different ways, it is necessary to give some background before considering how it has been applied to quality assurance.

Foucault's criticisms of Marxism

Michel Foucault is a challenging, multifaceted thinker whose work can be interpreted in many ways, but his main target as a critical philosopher from the 1960s to his death in 1984 was arguably the economistic assumptions of Marxism and the misguided belief that it was possible for intellectuals to overthrow the power of law and the state through leading a working-class revolutionary movement. Foucault, by contrast, argued in a similar way to Nietzsche and Weber that the rise of the state should concern us more than capitalism as an economic system, and that even here 'power' is not exercised by government institutions, such as parliaments or police forces, but is everywhere. We are shaped and influenced, for example, by the assumptions that have developed about madness, criminality or sexuality, to the extent that we take these for granted in our everyday lives. Although there are many ways of reading Foucault's ethical and philosophical project, it could be argued that he was generally pessimistic about the prospects for change in a managed, rationalised society. He believed, for example, that it was impossible and misguided to seek large-scale political change, and that progressive intellectuals had historically done great damage in exercising power over marginal or 'subjugated' groups such as prisoners or psychiatric patients (Foucault, 1980, p 82).

The governmentality tradition

The governmentality tradition has become popular in British and Australian sociology through the writing of Nikolas Rose, Peter Miller, Mitchell Dean, Pat O'Malley and others who have pursued, in a thoroughgoing manner, ideas outlined by Foucault in a lecture on the nature of government.[4] Foucault argued, in similar terms to Weber, that the state could be investigated independently from the economy as a set of ideas and institutions concerned with shaping 'the conduct of conduct' (Foucault, 1991). Rose and Miller (1992) have used this approach in studying the rise of neo-liberal government in Britain. They sometimes explicitly discuss quality assurance, although only as part of a wider set of changes in governance.

Rose and Miller's central argument was that, rather than being seen as confined to the activities of legislatures and government agencies, the state should be seen as encompassing 'many and varied alliances between political and other authorities that seek to govern economic activity, social life and individual conduct' (Rose and Miller, 1992, p 173). Key to this were the expert knowledges or 'governmental technologies' that had become part of government to the extent that it no longer made sense to distinguish between the state and civil society:

> Knowledge ... does not simply mean 'ideas' but refers to the vast assemblage of persons, theories, projects, experiments and techniques that has become such a central component of government. Theories from philosophy to medicine. Schemes from town-planning to social insurance. Techniques from double entry book-keeping to compulsory medical inspection of school-children. Knowledgeable persons from generals to architects and accountants. Our concern, that is to say, is with the 'know how' that has promised to make government possible. (Rose and Miller, 1992, p 178)

Through advancing this conception of government as a complex network of associations, they were challenging the still popular view advanced by Marxist thinkers that, if the economic conditions were right, the state could be overthrown or replaced in a political revolution. They were also arguing that the state could be understood sociologically, and not just by studying political history or philosophy:

> We need to study the humble and mundane mechanisms by which authorities seek to instantiate government: techniques of notation, computation and calculation; procedures of examination and assessment; the invention of devices such as surveys and presentational forms such as tables; the standardisation of systems for training and the inculcation of habits; the inauguration of professional specialisms and vocabularies; building designs and architectural forms – the list is heterogeneous and in principle unlimited. (Rose and Miller, 1992, p 183)

In this article, Rose and Miller also offered a preliminary analysis of 'welfarism' and 'neo-liberalism' as 'modes of government'. 'Welfarism' was an attempt by western societies 'to ensure high levels of employment, economic progress, social security, health and housing through ... state planning and intervention in the economy' (Rose and Miller, 1992, p 191). This meant creating large state bureaucracies staffed by technical experts. During the 1970s, there was, however, a shift to neo-liberalism that involved a significantly different way of thinking about government. From this perspective, attempts to redistribute income through high taxation were inflationary, since they often depended on 'currency depreciation' or 'public borrowing'. The welfare state was also harmful, since it created unhealthy dependence on benefits and was 'subject to constant pressure from bureaucrats to expand their own empires, again fuelling an expensive and inefficient extension of the governmental machine' (Rose and Miller, 1992, p 198). Neo-liberalism as a form of government has, therefore, aspired to reducing the size of the state through privatising services and agencies, and making bureaucracies subject to 'market principles'.

Although the last section might easily be read as a critique of neo-liberalism, in fact what is most striking, and in some respects most Foucauldian, about the statement as a whole is that Rose and Miller remained studiously neutral in talking about the political aspirations of welfarism and neo-liberalism. Governmentality theorists have been criticised, from within their own ranks, for withdrawing from politics into a form of scholasticism (O'Malley et al, 1997), which is perhaps an understandable response for left-wing intellectuals at a time when they feel increasingly isolated and have no political or intellectual strategy for combating neo-liberalism. This criticism fails to appreciate that Foucault's main target as a philosopher was not the misdoings of any particular government, but government itself; in other words, the modern state and its power to shape individuals. From this perspective, 'welfarism' and 'neo-liberalism' have much in common, not least that in each case government draws a great deal on the professions and expert knowledge.

A Foucauldian view of quality assurance

Rose and Miller did not mention quality assurance or auditing, although they commented on the emphasis placed on management in the Thatcher government's health service reforms. They noted, for example, that 'making people write things down, and the nature of things people are made to write down, is itself a kind of government of them, urging them to think about and note certain aspects of their activities according to certain norms' (Rose and Miller, 1992, p 200). There is a hint in this paragraph that they are critical of the flow of power towards managers 'who can compare and evaluate the activities of others who are merely entries on the chart'. However, no explicit criticisms or objections were advanced, which is consistent with the

Foucauldian view that all professionals and experts pose a problem to human freedom, not just 'experts of management'.

In a later analysis of neo-liberalism, Rose includes a paragraph about Power's work on the increased use of auditing in the public sector. He notes that 'the mechanisms of audit have become versatile ways of purporting to render accountable and judgeable the activity of professionals, managers, businessmen, politicians and many others' (Rose, 1996, p 351).[5] This may suggest that Rose disapproves of auditing in a similar way to Power. However, he also suggests that there might be some benefit:

> a politics of expertise also needs to recognise that such mechanisms may perhaps contain some innovative possibilities for contesting and reshaping the relations of power between experts and their subjects. (Rose, 1996, p 353)

Like Foucault, Rose is, therefore, most concerned with the plight of the 'abjected clients' of professionals (Rose, 1996, p 351), or more generally the effect on human beings of 'technologies of governance' in the modern world. It is difficult to read these core theoretical statements as making a political objection to quality assurance or even to neo-liberalism more generally, since there is no suggestion that there is an alternative means of organising society. This is why Foucault, like Weber, is a rather pessimistic thinker. They are critical of the modern world but without suggesting that one can return to a pre-industrial age without regulation or the dominance of science and rationality in our culture, or even that there is any way of making modern life more bearable.

Habermas and Luhmann on regulation

Although critical writers often draw on a combination of ideas from Marx, Foucault and Durkheim, there are a number of ways in which one can theorise about quality assurance from a critical perspective. Power, for example, draws on Beck's (1992) and Giddens' (1990) popular view of the late modern world as characterised by insecurity and anxiety in the face of risks caused by technological progress. Auditing is one response to this, along with risk management, but itself generates more anxiety. There are also two major contemporary social theorists who have written about regulation extensively: Jürgen Habermas and Niklas Luhmann. They are each systems theorists, who write at a high level of abstraction about the modern world. Habermas in his early work was more optimistic than Foucault on the prospects, or at least the possibility, of change. Luhmann, although equally abstract, and offering no political programme, offers an interesting analysis of the limitations of law in regulating different areas of social life.

The colonisation of the lifeworld

A central theme in Habermas' complex theory about the constitution of modern, industrialised societies is that the state provides stability in a market economy, but only at the expense of generating a perpetual crisis caused by the inability to satisfy the expectations of citizens in the delivery of public services. Habermas' most critical work was published in the 1970s and failed to predict the neo-liberal restructuring that has revitalised capitalism. Although governments do their best to pretend otherwise, it is clear that most public services are underfunded in relation to demand. It is significant that even the beneficiaries of moves towards a two-tier system (those who have private health insurance or can access good-quality education through moving to a middle-class area) often feel anxious or insecure. From this perspective, quality assurance could be seen as the latest attempt to overcome a 'legitimation crisis' (Habermas, 1973, 1987) by persuading a sceptical public that all is well, which inevitably generates further concerns.

More generally, Habermas argued that the modern state and 'juridification' were bad for individuals and social institutions in what he called the 'lifeworld'. In this passage, he suggests that the welfare state by the 1970s had become deeply unpopular through making people dependent on bureaucracy:

> The more the welfare state goes beyond pacifying the class conflict lodged in the sphere of production and spreads a net of client relationships over private spheres of life, the stronger are the anticipated pathological side effects of a juridification that entails both a bureaucratisation and a monetarisation of core areas of the lifeworld. The *dilemmatic structure* [emphasis in original] of this type of juridification consists in the fact that, while the welfare-state guarantees are intended to serve the goal of social integration, they nevertheless promote the disintegration of life-relations when these are separated, through legalized social intervention, from the consensual mechanisms that

coordinate action and are transferred over to media such as power and money. (Habermas, 1987, p 365)

There is a certain irony here in that New Right thinkers during the 1970s were making similar criticisms of bureaucracy, and a dissatisfaction with the welfare state was one factor behind the electoral success of neo-liberal governments. What seems equally interesting, however, is that despite government rhetoric and some degree of privatisation, the state today is even larger than during the 1970s. Here it is worth noting critically that the protest movements that interested Habermas were either labour unions organising to defend their conditions of work, or oppositional movements among the middle class such as the Campaign for Nuclear Disarmament. It is not clear from books like *Legitimation crisis* (Habermas, 1973) that there was a groundswell of discontent with bureaucracy. Although council tenants or hospital patients suffered from a deterioration of public services during the 1970s, they continued to support the welfare state. This is why British governments since the 1980s have reformed rather than attempted to abolish the social security system and National Health Service.

The limits of law

During the same period as Habermas was developing this critical theory, another German theorist, Niklas Luhmann, also considered the problem of bureaucracy and over-regulation (1985, 1995). They can each, to some extent, be understood as thinking through the analysis of modernity supplied by Durkheim and Parsons (discussed in Chapter Three). As society industrialises, it becomes more internally differentiated and dependent on technical experts, and this can create cultural and organisational problems. All these theorists are supporters of industrialisation, market economies, democratisation and the modern state, but are also aware of the dilemmas and contradictions. Habermas was an optimistic critic during the 1970s, who believed that the Enlightenment project could be completed to create a good society, based on science and open communication. Luhmann was arguably more pessimistic, or at least like Parsons he believed that we have to live with the problems of an evolving, complex society in which regulation can become ineffective and harmful (for discussion, see Haines and Sutton, 2003).

The objective in this book has been to stay close to the governmental institutions concerned with quality assurance and the organisations and people affected by these developments while resisting the temptation to theorise about regulation at a high level of abstraction. It will be apparent from the discussion of these academic critics that it is hard to separate a consideration of what quality assurance involves on the ground, and long-standing, philosophically driven debates about modernity. Luhmann does not write about the effect of particular laws or the relationship between different sub-systems of society in specific terms. However, his central argument about the 'autopoietic' character of all systems offers a useful way of understanding the place of law in society, and why regulation cannot be perfect.

Whereas the original dream of Enlightenment thinkers was that law could produce a rational, ordered world, Luhmann (1995) argues that the complexity of modern society makes this impossible. Although law has extended its reach to regulate ever more areas of social life, it cannot do this effectively. As Roger Cotterrell has suggested, from this theoretical perspective, 'its essential character as a communication system is ... one of ever-increasing technicality and complexity (mirroring the society for which it provides decisions) and immunity from any meaningful evaluation except in terms of this specifically legal technicality' (Cotterrell, 1992, p 168). Although this critique is directed against law as a body of specialist expertise and knowledge, it will be apparent that it can equally well apply to all state regulation. Quality assurance could, for example, be viewed as an autopoietic system with the objective of measuring professional work using scientific techniques, that has developed its own professional language. The difficulty arises that it may have only a limited effect on the areas of social life it seeks to regulate, or, as Power suggests, actually harm other sub-systems through inappropriate regulation. It is again worth noting that Luhmann does not offer any solution to the problem of juridification. He also views academic life as an autopoietic system that generates technical knowledge, but has lost the ability to communicate effectively with the rest of society.

How persuasive are the critics?

The immediate reaction of a hard-headed politician, civil servant or senior manager of a public sector agency in hearing the complaints of these academic commentators might be to dismiss them as hopelessly utopian or romantic. Most people in government believe that there is nothing sinister about using management and the application of scientific techniques to improve performance. Nor do they see anything problematic about capitalism: it is widely accepted that the economic problems of the 1970s required neo-liberal policies to open markets and make national economies more competitive (as Margaret Thatcher and Tony Blair have both argued, there is no alternative). The insecurity that public sector professionals, or workers in general, experience from periodic restructuring is seen as a good thing. It has, for example, been suggested that individuals benefit from constant change and having to learn new skills and sell themselves, rather than passively receiving a salary. There is also nothing wrong with quality assurance and auditing. After all, it does people good to reflect on what they are doing, and performance can always be improved. Finally, it should be noted that, from this perspective, leftist theorists such as Foucault have little to contribute to practical affairs. They are simply academic critics.

Perhaps the most effective response one can make to someone who believes in quality assurance or the dream of continuous improvement is to give concrete examples of how these initiatives affect organisations and individuals in practice, and also to remember that public services were delivered effectively during the 1970s without the need for mission statements, league tables and feedback forms. Having said this, it is important to recognise that how we respond to arguments or assess evidence ultimately depends on our basic values. There is also the problem that even if we agree on what makes a good society, there are usually contradictions and dilemmas that arise in trying to balance different kinds of rights. The remaining part of this chapter explores some of these issues in relation to academic arguments against quality assurance. It begins by contrasting the assumptions of supporters and critics of quality assurance, and suggests that the same debates have been pursued about the state and scientific management for more than 200 years. It then identifies a contradiction in the arguments of many critics, or a lack of clarity over where they stand on the issue of professional power.

A question of values

This chapter has demonstrated that the criticisms that can arise within a group of professionals about the burden of red tape are considerably more limited in scope than those made by theorists and philosophers who see quality assurance as one aspect of excessive rationalisation in the modern state.[6] One can, of course, argue that these wider questions are only of academic or intellectual interest, as opposed to the practical challenge of designing or implementing a quality assurance system. On the other hand, many managers would agree that before one can understand how an organisation works, and where it may be heading, it is necessary to know something about its history. Although this book has argued that quality assurance is a relatively recent development as a sub-field of management, from a broader historical perspective it is the latest chapter in the development of the modern state that has drawn on, and provided employment for, professional expertise of all kinds. This means that debates about the state and regulation conducted by sociologists over the past 200 years are all relevant to quality assurance.

Broadly speaking, there have been two main views. Like other Enlightenment thinkers, St Simon and Comte wanted democratic governments to replace the corrupt and despotic ancien régime (a battle that was not won in Europe until the second half of the 19th century). They also, however, believed that political change would enable forward-thinking governments to employ industrialists and scientific experts to produce a better world. Although it is not clear from their writings how scientific expertise should be used, they were impressed by the ability of modern governments to measure different aspects of society through collecting statistics in areas such as crime, mortality, family breakdown and health. By contrast, conservatives such as Edmund Burke and De Tocqueville at the time of the French Revolution, and German thinkers associated with the Romantic movement throughout the 19th century, have been suspicious about the ability of science to solve social problems, or believed that the growth of the state would create a new tyranny in which human beings were reduced to the state of happy robots, having given away their freedom to a scientific elite. Numerous thinkers, including Nietzsche and Weber, have taken issue with the view that we are happier or spiritually better off in an advanced industrial civilisation even though we live longer, lack for nothing materially, and have a bewildering choice of consumer goods.

With this background, one can see how quality assurance invites two moral responses. Modernisers and proponents of science have always believed in the principle of 'continuous improvement', and the extension of management into new areas of social life. By contrast, for romantics, quality assurance is the latest example of how the state over-regulates different areas of social life, and symptomatic of an unrealistic, and even arrogant, belief in scientific methods. One can see this distrust of science and the state informing the writings of Power and O'Neill, which are directed specifically towards quality assurance. This is even more apparent in the critiques of regulation made by Foucault, Habermas and Luhmann.

The problem of the professions

Although they share a distrust of quality assurance, it will be apparent that there are wide differences between the academic traditions reviewed in this chapter. O'Neill and Power argue that society needs to trust professionals and established institutions in similar terms to Durkheim. By contrast, Marxists and Foucauldians are considerably more ambivalent towards the moral claims of professionals, while also criticising managers and the state. The labour process tradition in Marxism views public sector professionals sympathetically as the latest group whose conditions of work have worsened under capitalism. Foucauldians, on the other hand, who could be described as the new Weberians, are deeply distrustful and ambivalent towards professionals, and more generally the role of expert knowledge in the modern world. However, like Weber, they see no prospects for change and no political programme is offered as an alternative to neo-liberalism.

In some respects, distinguishing between three separate traditions is helpful (and makes it possible to think more clearly about the issues). It can, however, also be misleading given that sociological writers often conflate the positions. It is common, for example, to find that critics complain about over-regulation in Foucauldian terms, while expressing unqualified support for the professions. An example can be found in a critique of quality assurance in higher education published in the influential collection edited by Marilyn Strathern (2000). This starts with what sounds like a Foucauldian critique:

> The French philosopher Foucault provides ample evidence of ways in which seemingly dull, routine and bureaucratic practices often have profound effects on social life. Our analysis underlies the fact that audit technologies being introduced into higher education and elsewhere are not simply innocuously neutral, legal-rational practices: rather they are instruments for new forms of governance and power. They embody a new rationality and morality and are designed to engender amongst academic staff new norms of conduct and professional behaviour. In short, they are agents for the creation of new kinds of subjectivity: self-managing individuals who render themselves auditable. (Shore and Wright, 2000, p 58)

They go on to discuss the effects of 'new categories of experts' such as quality assurers in regulating academics and changing how they think about professional practice:

> First, they develop a new expert knowledge and a discourse which create the classifications for a new framework or template of norms, a normative grid for the measurement and regulation of individual and organizational performance. Second, their grids of expertise are used for the design of institutional procedures for setting targets and assessing achievements. Third, certain of these experts staff and manage the new regulatory mechanisms and systems, and judge levels of compliance or deviance. Fourth, they have a therapeutic and redeeming role: they tutor individuals in the art of self-improvement and steer them towards desired norms. (Shore and Wright, 2000, p 62)

This is followed by a paragraph that discusses ways in which some professionals have resisted these initiatives, for example, 'by developing managerial competencies themselves' but 'in such a way as to enhance their professional status and clinical autonomy' (Shore and Wright, 2000, p 63). The rest of the chapter suggests that academics have not been successful in resisting this new form of regulation. This is because they can hardly ignore league tables or refuse to participate in the RAE. They are 'like managers ... caught in a disciplinary system whose negative characteristics they are actively producing, yet over which they feel increasingly powerless' (Shore and Wright, 2000, p 77).

Although this reads as a political argument against quality assurance, Shore and Wright offer no suggestions on what can be done to challenge managerialism in the public sector. They conclude by shifting from a Foucauldian to a Marxist register by suggesting that the root of the problem lies 'from the pressure on firms to obtain ever-greater profits and productivity from the workforce' (Shore and Wright, 2000, p 85). However, at no point is there any consideration that expert knowledge might itself be viewed as a problem. Foucault constantly draws our attention to the fact that academics, along with other professionals, are fully implicated in creating, administering and benefiting from technologies of governance. Marx's admittedly utopian vision of a society where the state has 'withered away' does not include a role for professionals, and he sees the split between manual and mental labour as a key element of alienation. By contrast, these authors and many others who have drawn on Marx or Foucault seem to be offering an unqualified defence of professionals against greater state regulation in the same way as O'Neill. They do not consider the power exercised over ordinary citizens by professionals, whether it might be desirable to reduce our dependence on experts, and, if so, how this might be achieved.

The success of quality assurance as a social movement in recent times means that it has no need to engage with its intellectual critics. A steady stream of theorists and commentators has written about managerialism and the consequences of over-regulation, but no one in government has taken this seriously. One can also see, however, that the critics are vulnerable to the charge that they are simply defending the traditional economic interests and privileges of the professions. It is hard to criticise the idea that doctors or teachers should listen to the views of patients and students (increasingly described as 'consumers' rather than 'clients') without sounding arrogant or elitist. Ironically, sociologists criticised powerful professional groups like doctors, psychiatrists and teachers during the 1960s, and some even suggested the need for greater regulation (Freidson, 1975). This makes it difficult to complain when the same systems and procedures are extended to university teaching and research. Aside from O'Neill, few academic critics have argued that professionals should be trusted to practise without outside interference as in the old days, so it is not always clear what alternative is being suggested to quality assurance.

Notes

[1] For discussion of recent developments, see Kirkpatrick et al (2005), and contributors to Ackroyd et al (1995) and Ferlie et al (2005).

[2] Thompson (1983) has argued that the main arguments have been 'absorbed' into general sociology.

[3] One advantage of the Foucauldian tradition is that it allows leftist sociologists to write about cultural issues, such as how the body is regulated, which was not possible within economistic versions of Marxism (Kendall and Wickham, 2001).

[4] See, for example, Rose (1993, 1996), Rose and Miller (1992), Dean (1999), O'Malley (2000).

[5] Through using the word 'purported', Rose makes it clear that, like other governmentality theorists, he is not interested in the success or

failure of governmental programmes, but only in mapping out how programmes and technologies change over time (see also Dean, 1999).

[6] A central theme in Weber's writings is that modern life is organised by rules and regulations: every institution, from the economy to law and even music, is over-rationalised (see Hughes et al, 1995, ch 3).

EIGHT

Conclusion: learning to live with regulation

Best Value or social pathology?
Assessing the evidence
The inevitability of regulation

What makes quality assurance interesting as a sociological topic is that, although it is politically secure, and taken for granted as the only way to manage the public services, there are still widely differing views about this new form of regulation. On the one hand, there are the certainties of government, as illustrated in speeches during the late 1990s by Tony Blair, about the need for constant improvement in the delivery of public services, and the matter-of-fact, institutionalised character of quality assurance described in Chapters Four and Five. Then there are the frustrations experienced by professionals on the ground considered in Chapters Three and Six and the broader criticisms of academics summarised and discussed in Chapter Seven, which are partly cultural criticisms of the role of science and regulation in the modern world.

As Herbert Blumer (1971, p 299) noted in the early 1970s, 'the vast over-organisation that is developing in modern society' is not generally viewed as a political issue. Right-wing parties and business groups complain about over-regulation, but accept the need for a strong state. Progressive thinkers, including sociologists who write books about the problems of modernity, are worried about growing levels of economic inequality and insecurity within and between nation states, as well as damage to the environment and the cultural problems of rampant individualism. Few social critics since Max Weber have, however, focused on the growth of bureaucracy and regulation as a political, social or cultural problem.

Nevertheless, there is a debate taking place about quality assurance. This partly relates to whether we trust professionals, like doctors, teachers or lawyers, or believe that they require greater regulation. More fundamentally, however, it raises difficult issues about whether 'continuous improvement' (the great dream of the modern period) is possible, and whether one can measure everything using scientific procedures. This concluding chapter reviews the two sides of the argument (quality assurance and its critics) and considers the extent to which evidence of the kind supplied about what measuring quality actually involves, and how it is experienced by professionals and organisations, can resolve this kind of political or moral argument. Given that quality assurance is not only established but institutionalised in the management of public services, and seems unlikely to disappear for the foreseeable future, the chapter concludes with some observations about the inevitability of regulation.

Best Value or social pathology?

Senior managers in public sector agencies are already aware of the problems created by quality assurance, such as the expense involved in preparing for multiple inspections. They know that league tables, or performance measures such as the numbers on hospital waiting lists, do not tell the whole story about whether an organisation is successful. They are also sympathetic to the burdens created by over-regulation and assessment, and do their best to minimise these while satisfying the requirements imposed by central government. However, they still broadly accept that quality can be measured, and believe that 'continuous improvement' is possible through exercising leadership. In these circumstances, quality assurance represents what one government initiative described as 'Best Value': it achieves a variety of objectives at an acceptable cost. Many managers and professionals (they are often the same people) also believe that quality assurance is valuable, and that professional work requires greater regulation to maintain and raise standards.

On the other side of the debate are disgruntled professionals who have to spend a large proportion of their time on administration, and are constantly told that they cannot be trusted to do a good job without supervision. They often complain about the unnecessary and burdensome work of quality assurance (its 'ridiculous' character). General practitioners, teachers, police officers and legal aid lawyers resent having to produce documents and reports that do not describe the actual, practical circumstances of their work or address what they feel is important. Producing these documents eats into their time and can even affect the quality of their work. To return to the example of feedback forms, a teacher who takes student comments too seriously will not take risks: but if promotion depends on getting good scores, it is hard not to be influenced by regulation. They can also affect the character of the student–teacher relationship: there is a big difference between asking for informal feedback when this seems appropriate, and a system where forms with official warnings about rights and obligations are administered on a regular basis. This not only creates bureaucracy and 'juridification', but also changes the character of the student–teacher relationship, at least on the day the form is administered.

Critics often combine a dislike of red tape with objections to the amount of money spent on management and administration, which has steadily increased since the 1980s. The evidence for this is compelling. Hood et al (1999, p 25), after a careful review of the 'regulatory state', estimate that 'the number of regulator organizations in the national public sector runs from about 130 to over 200 and our estimate of the direct running costs from about £700m. at the lower end to about £1bn. at the top end'. They also provide some disturbing figures about the costs of compliance that are not normally measured or assessed by regulatory agencies:

> For one inner London borough, we estimated the 'narrow' compliance costs of dealing with central government departments, inspectorates, ombudsmen, and local audit bodies as not less than £1.85m. per year. If that figure is extrapolated to all local authorities in England, using Treasury ... analyses of spending profiles, the total compliance costs for local government of dealing with their regulators would amount to no less than £173m. for England as a whole, or about 30p in every £100 spent by local government. Figures from the former Department of the Environment ... suggest the costs to local government in England of providing information required by its central-government regulators would run to at least £30m. per year. OFSTED inspection of secondary schools has been estimated to cost each school around £20,000 in expenses directly connected to inspection, and these costs rise further if, as in some cases, the LEA [local education authority] mounts a 'mock' inspection before the OFSTED visitation.... Putting such pieces of information together, it seems safe to conclude that compliance costs even in the narrow sense used above make the total cost of regulation inside UK government at least double the sum directly spent on the main regulatory bureaucracies. (Hood et al, 1999, p 27)

Power concluded his critique of the growth of auditing by complaining about the gulf between 'highly rewarded 'observing' and poorly rewarded 'doing'' (Power, 1997, p 147), and many public service professionals have concerns that their pay has declined in relationship to the private sector and that they are not properly appreciated. There is a widespread view among public sector professionals, sometimes expressed in union meetings, that whole tiers of middle management could be removed without affecting the quality of services. This view is, of course, easier to hold if you do not have management responsibilities. It is also a political issue in that thousands of new administrative and managerial jobs have been created by greater investment in public services during the three terms of a New Labour government.

Assessing the evidence

This study has provided an overview of debates in sociology, socio-legal studies and public administration about quality assurance, the professions and the regulatory state, rather than supplying a detailed ethnographic study of professional relations or the labour process in particular institutions or organisations. Nevertheless, it has drawn on empirical evidence, including interviews with quality assurers and professionals, case studies of systems and processes, and the analysis of documents. Some sections have described some of the practical tasks involved in completing forms and attempting to gain permission to study regulatory agencies. Those who prefer statistical evidence might regard these sections as anecdotal, but from an interpretive perspective they provide access to how we experience bureaucracy in everyday life.

There are, of course, many ways of employing qualitative methods and this study might fruitfully be contrasted in terms of methodological assumptions with critical studies in the labour process tradition, discussed in Chapter Seven, or the growing field of institutional ethnography (Smith, 2005; Rankin and Campbell, 2006). Rather than advancing a political argument, based on a scientific claim to know more about the structure, workings and political choices in society than managers or professionals, this study has pursued the more modest objective of describing a number of perspectives, the practical work involved in making quality judgements, and how quality assurance affects people in their working lives.[1] The chapters based on empirical research convey the difficulties that arise in trying to measure performance objectively, the sheer amount of work involved in maintaining the system of regulation, and the frustrations experienced by professionals.

Chapter Three describes some aspects of the situated, practical skills and knowledge employed in legal practice. Once one starts to appreciate what these skills involve, even by looking at a short transcript of a lawyer giving professional advice, it becomes apparent that the exercise of judgement in particular situations cannot easily be measured using quantitative indicators. As suggested in a previous article, attempts to measure quality in legal work through client satisfaction surveys bear little relationship to how lawyers understand competence (Travers, 1994). This is not presented as a great discovery, but as something everyone already knows, even though it is not acknowledged by politicians or public sector managers who increasingly rely on surveys to demonstrate performance. It explains why professionals often describe quality assurance as 'ridiculous'.

Chapters Four and Five provide some detail on the sheer amount of work created by quality assurance as a form of regulation. They describe the work of inspectors making quality judgements about public sector agencies, which involves lengthy meetings to decide whether the evidence supplied in documents and 'reality checks' supports findings and recommendations for improvement. This careful, methodical work is being conducted in numerous inspectorates across the public sector, resulting in thousands of reports being posted on websites each year. Although it is hard to study at close quarters, owing to the sensitivity of the institutions being inspected, there is something remarkable about the amount of time and effort spent in assessing the quality of public sector management. One question that has already been addressed in a government review (Office of Public Services Reform, 2003) is whether all this is really necessary, or whether the same result could be achieved at less public expense.

Chapter Five looks at the systems employed in measuring quality in three organisations, a 'new' and 'old' university and a police force. These demonstrate that, in addition to bureaucratic record keeping, a large amount of administrative work is concerned with measuring quality. Those working in the public sector will already know about, and perhaps take for granted, the elaborate systems employed in auditing. It still, however, seems remarkable that so much time is spent each year producing reports, attending meetings and documenting achievements annually to show objectives and outcomes, making it possible to 'tick the boxes' and demonstrate 'continuous improvement' the following year. The overlapping systems of accountability in a police force, and the resigned but good-humoured responses of the quality managers who have to produce the reports, also seem characteristic of how British institutions currently work. Although it is difficult obtaining figures from government or the agencies themselves, one can see from these case studies that a significant number of administrators are employed to satisfy external demands for accountability.

Chapter Six looks at the responses of professionals to quality assurance. There are methodological difficulties in that an interview or survey can both exaggerate and understate the frustrations caused by administrative procedures. One finding is that some professionals do not view quality assurance as a problem. Those who do seem equally concerned about the growth of administration and red tape that may not be related to quality assurance. There is, however, evidence that all these complaints are connected with a more generalised unease about changes in public sector work and the reduced status and influence of professionals. There is resentment towards managers for no longer trusting them to act competently or in the best interests of clients who are increasingly understood as consumers. One small example is that in appraisal interviews in some universities, lecturers are asked to supply statistical information from feedback questionnaires to document whether they have achieved their annual objectives for teaching. During the 1970s, they would have been trusted to assess their own performance.

Although these accounts of different perspectives and procedures are helpful in providing some information about the impact of quality assurance on public sector work, they are not intended as evidence that can answer political questions. Given that governments and other agencies currently place great faith in evidence-based policy, this might sound like a provocative or disturbing statement, or perhaps one that leads to the nihilistic belief that there is no such thing as truth (Wiles, 2002). No one can, however, dispute that there are usually different ways of interpreting facts. One would not expect someone committed to the idea of 'continuous improvement' to become disheartened by the fact that the same problems regularly resurface in organisations, or that regulation can be burdensome. Similarly, one would not expect a critic to become converted to the merits of inspection and auditing through spending time with managers and inspectors. As in any other political dispute, there are vested interests involved as well as conflicts between deeply rooted values.

No amount of evidence will, therefore, persuade anyone who believes that quality assurance improves performance or prevents misconduct or incompetence to accept that we could do without it, or that the cure is worse than the illness. However, I would argue that, if civil servants and government ministers take evidence-based policy seriously, it is worth considering whether this aspect of the new public sector management has been an unqualified success. At the very least, one can see both costs and benefits in measuring quality, and perhaps it is time to recognise that there are significant costs.

The inevitability of regulation

As discussed in Chapter Seven, sociologists face a difficulty in responding to quality assurance and regulation in its broader sense in that sociology itself began as a scientific project concerned with improving the world through the application of human reason. This remains a central aspiration even though other sociologists have shared with the Romantic movement a distrust of, or ambivalence towards, science and the state. This is why the humble feedback form, and the procedures around it, can arouse strong feelings: it promises 'continuous improvement' (the Enlightenment belief in progress) and yet can be viewed as shackling human spontaneity and freedom. What is particularly interesting is that we mostly take this form of assessment for granted, along with quality management in general, whereas it has only existed since the 1980s. This raises the question as to whether quality assurance is inevitable or whether it may prove a relatively short-lived management fashion, or even a fad (Best, 2006).

The social sciences have amply demonstrated that they cannot predict the future, but they have done well in identifying general tendencies in the modern world. One of these has been the growth of the state and legal regulation, which shows no signs of slowing, and indeed may be accelerating. David Marquand (2004, p 133) has noted that 'the state of the early twenty-first century is incomparably bigger, more centralised and more complex than that of the nineteenth'. He has also identified the paradox that neo-liberals in both the Thatcher and New Labour governments have required a strong, centralised state to promote free-market economics (Marquand, 2004, pp 97-100). An equally significant development has been the contraction of manufacturing industry owing to automation and globalisation, with the result that a large proportion of the workforce in advanced, industrialised countries is employed as professionals, managers and administrators. As many social theorists have pointed out, the human sciences and innumerable forms of applied knowledge and expertise developed during this period. This process also appears to be accelerating, so one could argue that human beings have never been more subject to expert knowledges and fine-grained regulation. Quality assurance is simply another example of how rational, scientific methods are used to manage and improve human beings, and it would be foolish to think we could challenge or replace it.

The most systematic attempt to explain the emphasis on measurement and evaluation by neo-liberal governments in the past two decades has been made by writers in the Foucauldian governmentality tradition. They have argued, primarily by analysing policy documents, that the shift from Keynesian to monetarist economic management and the increasing emphasis placed on self-regulation ('government at a distance') are connected. They are presented as part of an emerging new 'episteme', the latest stage of liberal governance, usually in a way that gives the analyst some critical leverage by contrasting governance in our own times with post-war social democracy. Many theorists who write about bureaucracy in these terms owe an unacknowledged debt to Weber, who wrote pessimistically about the growth of the state in late 19th-century Germany. Weber accepted that bureaucracy was technically superior to other forms of organisation, but was concerned that it contributed to a world where everything was known and measured. He also noted presciently that 'once it is fully established, bureaucracy is among those social structures which are hardest to destroy', not least because 'compliance has been conditioned into the officials ... and the governed' (Weber, 1991, pp 228-9).[2]

A problem with this type of critical analysis (along with conservative theorising about the 'end of history') is that it does not differentiate between different types of bureaucracy, or how institutions and whole societies change, and might lead one to view quality assurance as an inevitable feature of modernity. In fact, one could equally well argue that it has only been successful owing to a particular set of economic and political circumstances, and has only really flourished as a form of regulation in Britain. Chapter One suggests that quality assurance has many of the characteristics of a social movement that has spread from America to Britain in response to concerns felt in government, and among the public, about poor performance in the delivery of public services. According to Marquand, it is also closely connected with the neo-liberal political parties that have been electorally successful in recent times. These have aggressively promoted market values and attempted to undermine the service ethic associated with the professions (Marquand, 2004, pp 2-3). Much of the work involved in promoting and building the movement during the 1980s took place behind closed doors, so it is difficult to identify how it developed. What does seem evident is that quality assurance started, like many movements, with missionary zeal promising to transform the world, but has since become institutionalised as bureaucratic regulation.

Once established, any regulatory system quickly acquires a taken-for-granted character but it also has the full weight of organisational sanctions behind it, so there are real consequences for refusing to administer a feedback form. One might also add that institutions and organisations maintain and reproduce themselves through groups and individuals unreflectively following rules and procedures. Most students complete compulsory anonymous feedback forms, almost as a ritual after each course, without having any suggestions to make, or expecting that any changes will follow. For their lecturers, the processing of the information becomes an administrative task disconnected from the other measures taken to improve courses through exercising professional judgement. This means that quality assurance seems likely to be around for a long time, owing to the sheer weight of institutional or bureaucratic momentum. But it also means that no one really believes that completing a feedback form every year will deliver 'continuous improvement', and the system will not last forever.

The other problem with viewing quality assurance as inevitable is that it only exists, in its developed form, in Britain and other European countries with a large public sector. Although the issue of giving up sovereignty and the pound remains a politically contentious one, in many respects Britain is already regulated by the European Union (Hood et al, 1999, ch 8; Pollitt and Bouckaert, 2004). This is one reason why we can expect a continuing emphasis on evaluation and regulation in public life in future governments. However, this is not necessarily true for the rest of the world. Although it is difficult to make comparisons, there appears to be less concern about public sector regulation among professionals in America than in Britain. If one looks further afield in the developing world, where the state is often weak, the problem may be that there is a shortage of managers and too little bureaucracy.[3]

In Australia, which has a small state by British standards, there are currently only two independent inspectorates, and nothing like the same emphasis on auditing and setting targets. Some Australian pioneers of quality management would argue that these are desperately needed, particularly in the area of health. However, one could equally well ask why agencies in Australia appear to function perfectly well with less regulation. Against that, most graduates in social sciences are employed in administrative or managerial jobs, so one can hardly object, as a sociologist, to the creation of new inspectorates. It is hard to avoid the conclusion that quality assurance will continue to grow as an occupation. Perhaps the critics must learn to live with this form of regulation along with other disagreeable features of the modern world.

Notes

[1] For similar interpretive studies, see Harper (2000), Wiener (2000) and Timmermans and Berg (2003).

[2] For a summary of Weber's views on bureaucracy, see Sayer (1991, ch 4).

[3] This point was made by a management consultant during a session on new forms of regulation at the 2006 World Congress of Sociology, Durban, South Africa.

References

Abbott, A. (1988) *The system of professions: An essay on the division of expert labour*, Chicago, IL: University of Chicago Press.

Ackroyd, S., Batt, R., Thompson, P. and Tolbert, P. (eds) (1995) *The Oxford handbook of work and organisation*, Oxford: Oxford University Press.

Agger, B. (2000) *Public sociology: From social facts to literary acts*, Lanham, MD: Rowman and Littlefield.

Associated Press (2005) 'America's trade deficit hits all-time high' (www.msnbc.msn.com/id/11270337).

Atkinson, P. (1997) *The clinical experience: The construction and reconstruction of medical reality*, Aldershot: Ashgate.

Audit Commission (1989) *Managing services effectively: Performance review*, Audit Commission Management Paper no 5, London: HMSO.

Audit Commission (1992) *Local authority performance indicators*, London: HMSO.

Audit Commission (1993) *Putting quality on the map: Measuring and appraising quality in the public service*, London: HMSO.

Baker, K. (1993) *The turbulent years*, London: Faber and Faber.

Banks, G. (2003) 'The good, the bad and the ugly: economic perspectives on regulation in Australia', Address to the Conference of Economists, Hyatt Hotel, Canberra, 2 October.

Baty, P. (2004) 'Academic happy to quit dog's life', *Times Higher Education Supplement*, 30 July, p 3.

Beck, U. (1992) *Risk society*, London: Sage Publications.

Becker, H. (1963) *Outsiders: Studies in the sociology of deviance*, New York, NY: The Free Press.

Becker, H., Hughes, E., Geer, B. and Strauss, A. (1961) *Boys in white: Student culture in a medical school*, Chicago, IL: University of Chicago Press.

Berk, J. and Berk, S. (1993) *Total quality management: Implementing continuous improvement*, New York, NY: Sterling.

Berman, M. (1983) *All that is solid melts into air: The experience of modernity*, London: Verso.

Best, J. (ed) (1995) *Images of issues: Typifying contemporary social problems*, New York, NY: Walter de Gruyter.

Best, J. (2006) *Flavor of the month: Why smart people fall for fads*, Berkeley, CA: University of California Press.

Better Regulation Task Force (2002) *Higher education: Easing the burden*, London: Cabinet Office.

Better Regulation Task Force (2005) *Less is more. Reducing burdens, improving outcomes*, London: Cabinet Office.

Bittner, E. (1963) 'Radicalism and the organisation of radical movements', *American Sociological Review*, vol 28, no 6, pp 928-40.

Blumer, H. (1971) 'Social problems as collective behaviour', *Social Problems*, vol 18, no 3, pp 298-306.

Bourdieu, P. (1990) *In other words: Essays towards a reflexive sociology*, Cambridge: Polity.

Braverman, H. (1974) *Labour and monopoly capitalism: The degradation of work in the twentieth century*, London: Monthly Review Press.

Brint, S. (1994) *In an age of experts: The changing role of professionals in politics and public life*, Princeton, NJ: Princeton University Press.

Burawoy, M. (2005) 'For public sociology: the 2004 American sociological association presidential address', *British Journal of Sociology*, vol 56, no 2, pp 259-94.

Burchell, G., Gordon, C. and Miller, P. (1991) *The Foucault effect: Studies in governmentality*, London: Harvester Wheatsheaf.

Cabinet Office (1992) *The Citizen's Charter*, London: HMSO.

Cabinet Office (2005) 'Public services inspection' (www.cabinetoffice.gov.uk/regulation/reviewing_regulation/public_services_inspection/index.asp, accessed 1 March 2006).

Carr-Saunders, P. and Wilson, P. (1933) *The professions*, Oxford: Clarendon Press.

Carter, N., Klein, R. and Day, P. (1992) *How organisations measure success: The use of performance indicators in government*, London: Routledge.

Chestnut, B. (1997) *Quality assurance: An Australian guide to ISO 9000 certification*, Melbourne: Longman.

Cicourel, A. (1976) *The social organisation of juvenile justice*, London: Heinemann.

Clegg, S. (1990) *Modern organisations: Organisation studies in the modern world*, London: Sage Publications.

Cohen, L., Wilkinson, A., Arnold, J. and Finn, R. (2005) "Remember I'm the bloody architect!' Architects, organisations and discourses of production', *Work, Employment and Society*, vol 19, no 4, pp 775-96.

Collins, H. and Pinch, T. (1982) *Frames of meaning: The social construction of extraordinary science*, London: Routledge.

Collins, R. (1979) *The credential society: A historical sociology of education and stratification*, New York, NY: Academic Press.

Cooke, H. (2006) 'Seagull management and the control of nursing work', *Work, Employment and Society*, vol 20, no 2, pp 223-43.

Cotterrell, R. (1992) *The sociology of law: An introduction*, London: Butterworths.

Crosby, P. (1979) *Quality is free*, New York, NY: New American Library.

Cuff, E., Sharrock, W. and Francis, D. (2006) *Perspectives in sociology*, London: Routledge.

Davies, H., Nutley, S. and Smith, P. (eds) (2000) *What works? Evidence-based policy and practice in public services*, Bristol: The Policy Press.

Day, P. and Klein, R. (1990) *Inspecting the inspectorates: Services for the elderly*, York: Joseph Rowntree Memorial Trust.

Dean, M. (1999) *Governmentality: Power and rule in modern society*, London: Sage Publications.

Dearing, R. (1997) *Higher education in the learning society*, London: National Committee of Inquiry into Higher Education.

Deleuze, G. (1995) *Negotiations 1972–1990*, New York, NY: Columbia University Press.

Deming, W.E. (1986) *Out of the crisis: Quality, productivity and competitive production*, Cambridge: Cambridge University Press.

Derrida, J. (1978) *Writing and difference*, Chicago, IL: University of Chicago Press.

DES (Department of Education and Science) (1991) *The Parent's Charter*, London: HMSO.

De Toqueville, A. (2003) *Democracy in America*, Harmondsworth: Penguin.

Du Gay, P. (2000) *In praise of bureaucracy*, London: Sage Publications.

Durkheim, E. (1959) *Socialism and Saint-Simon*, London: Routledge and Kegan Paul.

Durkheim, E. (1984) *The division of labour in society*, London: Macmillan.

Easthope, C. and Easthope, G. (2000) 'Intensification, extension and complexity of teachers' workload', *British Journal of the Sociology of Education*, vol 21, no 1, pp 43-58.

Ebel, K. (1991) *Achieving excellence in business: A practical guide to the total quality transformation process*, Milwaukee, NY: ASQC Quality Press.

Ellis, R. (ed) (1988) *Professional competence and quality assurance in the caring professions*, London: Chapman and Hall.

Exworthy, M. and Halford, S. (eds) (1998) *Professionals and the new managerialism in the public sector*, Milton Keynes: Open University Press.

Fairclough, N. (2000) *New labour, new language?*, London: Routledge.

Ferlie, E., Lynn, L. and Pollitt, C. (eds) (2005) *The Oxford handbook of public management*, Oxford: Oxford University Press.

Fitz-Gibbon, C. and Stephenson-Forster, N. (1999) 'Is Ofsted helpful?', in C. Cullingford (ed) *An inspector calls: Ofsted and its effect on school standards*, London: Kogan Page, pp 97-118.

Foucault, M. (1967) *Madness and civilisation: A history of insanity in the age of reason*, London: Tavistock.

Foucault, M. (1977) *Discipline and punish: The birth of the prison*, London: Tavistock.

Foucault, M. (1980) 'Truth and power', in C. Gordon (ed) *Power-knowledge: Selected interviews and other writings*, New York, NY: Pantheon, pp 109-33.

Foucault, M. (1991) 'Governmentality', in G. Burchall, C. Gordon and P. Miller (eds) *The Foucault effect: Studies in governmentality*, London: Harvester Wheatsheaf.

Francis, D. and Hester, S. (2004) *An invitation to ethnomethodology: Language, society and interaction*, London: Sage Publications.

Freidson, E. (1970) *Professional dominance: The social structure of medical care*, New York, NY: Atherton Press.

Freidson, E. (1975) *Doctoring together: A study of professional social control*, New York, NY: Elsevier.

Freidson, E. (1984) 'The changing nature of professional control', *Annual Review of Sociology*, vol 10, pp 1-10.

Freidson, E. (1994) *Professionalism reborn: Theory, prophecy and policy*, Chicago, IL: University of Chicago Press.

Freidson, E. (2001) *Professionalism: The third logic*, Cambridge: Polity Press.

Fulton, J. (1968) *The civil service: Report of the committee*, London: HMSO.

Furedi, F. (2004) *Where have all the intellectuals gone? Confronting 21st century philistinism*, New York, NY: Continuum.

Garfinkel, H. (1984) *Studies in ethnomethodology*, Cambridge: Polity Press.

Garfinkel, H. (1997) 'Practical sociological reasoning: some features in the work of the Los Angeles suicide prevention center', in M. Travers and J. Manzo (eds) *Law in action: Ethnomethodological and conversation analytic approaches to law*, Aldershot: Ashgate, pp 25-42.

Garfinkel, H. (2002) *Ethnomethodology's program*, Lanham, MD: Rowman and Littlefield.

Garfinkel, H. and Wieder, D. (1991) 'Two incommensurably asymmetrically alternate technologies of social analysis', in G. Watson and R. Seiler (eds) *Text in context: Contributions to ethnomethodology*, London: Sage Publications, pp 175-206.

Garvin, D. (1991) 'How the Baldridge award actually works', *Harvard Business Review*, Nov-Dec, pp 80-93.

Gaster, L. (1995) *Quality in public services: Managers' choices*, Milton Keynes: Open University Press.

Gaster, L. and Squires, A. (1993) *Providing quality in the public sector*, Milton Keynes: Open University Press.

Giddens, A. (1990) *The consequences of modernity*, Cambridge: Polity Press.

Giddens, A. (1994) *Beyond left and right: The future of radical politics*, Cambridge: Polity Press.

Glidewell, I. (1998) *Review of the Crown Prosecution Service*, London: HMSO.

Goffman, E. (1959) *The presentation of self in everyday life*, Garden City, NY: Doubleday.

Goffman, E. (1961) *Asylums*, Harmondsworth: Penguin.

Goffman, E. (1967) 'Where the action is', in E. Goffman, *Interaction ritual: Essays on face to face behavior*, Garden City, NY: Doubleday, pp 149-270.

Goodsell, C. (1983) *The case for bureaucracy: A public administration polemic*, Chatham, NJ: Chatham House Publishers.

Gouldner, A. (1952) 'Red-tape as social problem', in R. Merton, A. Gray, B. Hockey and H. Selvin et al (eds) *Reader in bureaucracy*, New York, NY: The Free Press, pp 410-18.

Gouldner, A. (1971) *The coming crisis of western sociology*, Heinemann: London.

Gouldner, A. (1979) *The future of intellectuals and the rise of the New Class*, London: Macmillan.

Grint, K. (1995) *Management: A sociological introduction*, Cambridge: Cambridge University Press.

Habermas, J. (1973) *Legitimation crisis*, Boston, MA: Beacon Press.

Habermas, J. (1987) *The theory of communicative action/Vol.2, Lifeworld and system: A critique of functionalist reason*, Cambridge: Polity Press.

Haines, F. and Sutton, A. (2003) 'The engineer's dilemma: a sociological perspective on juridification and regulation', *Crime, Law and Social Change*, vol 39, pp 1-22.

Harper, R. (1989) 'An ethnography of accountants', Unpublished PhD thesis, University of Manchester.

Harper, R. (2000) 'The social organisation of the IMF's mission work: an examination of international auditing', in M. Strathern (ed) *Audit cultures: Anthropological studies in accountability, ethics and the academy*, London: Routledge, pp 21-54.

Harris, J. (1998) 'Scientific management, bureau professionalism, new managerialism: the labour process of state social work', *British Journal of Social Work*, vol 28, no 6, pp 839-62.

Harrison, S. and Dowswell, G. (2002) 'Autonomy and bureaucratic accountability in primary care: what English general practitioners say', *Sociology of Health and Illness*, vol 24, no 2, pp 208-26.

Hayek, F. (1976) *The road to serfdom*, London: Routledge.

Heller, J. (1994) *Catch 22*, London: Vintage.

Hood, C., Scott, C., Oliver, J., Jones, G. and Travers, T. (1999) *Regulation inside government: Waste-watchers, quality police and sleaze-busters*, Oxford: Oxford University Press.

Hughes, E. (1971) *The sociological eye*, Chicago, IL: Aldine.

Hughes, J., Martin, P. and Sharrock, W. (1995) *Understanding Classical Sociology*, London: Sage.

Hutton, W. (1995) *The state we're in*, London: Jonathan Cape.

Illich, I. (ed) (1973) *Disabling professions*, London: Boyar.

Kendall, G. and Wickham, G. (2001) *Understanding culture: Cultural studies, order, ordering*, London: Sage Publications.

Kennedy, I., Howard, R., Jarman, B. and Mclean, M. (2001) *Learning from Bristol: The report of the public inquiry into children's heart surgery at the Bristol Royal Infirmary 1984-1995*, London: HMSO.

Kirkpatrick, I. and Martinez Lucio, M. (eds) (1995) *The politics of quality in the public sector*, London: Routledge.

Kirkpatrick, I., Ackroyd, S. and Walker, R. (2005) *The new managerialism and public service professions: Change in health, social services and housing*, Basingstoke: Palgrave Macmillan.

Klandermans, B. and Staggenborg, S. (2002) *Methods of social movements research*, Minneapolis, MN: University of Minnesota Press.

Kuhn, T. (1962) *The structure of scientific revolutions*, Chicago, IL: University of Chicago Press.

Johnson, T. (1972) *Professions and power*, London: Macmillan.

Larson, M. (1977) *The rise of professionalism: A sociological analysis*, Berkeley, CA: University of California Press.

Latour, B. (1995) *Re-assembling the social: An introduction to actor-network-theory*, Oxford: Oxford University Press.

Latour, B. and Woolgar, S. (1986) *Laboratory life: The construction of scientific facts*, Princeton, NJ: Princeton University Press.

Lipsky, M. (1980) *Street level bureaucracy: Dilemmas of the individual in public services*, New York, NY: Russell Sage Foundation.

Lynch, M. (1985) *Art and artefact in laboratory science: A study of shop work and shop talk in a research laboratory*, London: Routledge.

Luhmann, N. (1985) *A sociological theory of law*, London: Routledge.

Luhmann, N. (1995) *Social systems*, Stanford, CA: University of Stanford Press.

Marquand, D. (2004) *Decline of the public: The hollowing out of citizenship*, Cambridge: Polity Press.

Marx, K. and Engels, F. (1979) *The communist manifesto* (first published 1848), Harmondsworth: Penguin.

Mauss, A. (1975) *Social problems as social movements*, Philadelphia, PA: Lippincott.

Maynard, D. (2003) *Bad news, good news: Conversational order in everyday talk and clinical settings*, Chicago, IL: University of Chicago Press.

Merton, R. (1952) 'Bureaucratic structure and personality', in R. Merton, A. Gray, B. Hockey and H. Selvin et al (eds) *Reader in bureaucracy*, New York, NY: The Free Press, pp 361-71.

Meyer, J. and Rowan, B. (1991) 'Institutionalised organizations: formal structure as myth and ceremony', in W. Powell and P. DiMaggio (eds) *The new institutionalism in organizational analysis*, Chicago, IL: University of Chicago Press, pp 41-62.

Michels, R. (1959) *Political parties: A sociological study of the oligarchical tendencies of modern democracy*, New York, NY: Dover Publications.

Milakovich, M. (1995) *Improving service quality: Achieving high performance in the public and private sectors*, Delray Beach, FL: St. Lucie Press.

Mills, C. Wright (1951) *White collar: The American middle classes*, New York, NY: Oxford University Press.

Mintzberg, H. (1973) *The nature of managerial work*, New York, NY: Harper and Row.

Mulberg, J. (2000) 'Cash for answers: the association between school performance and local government finance', Sociological Research Online, vol 5, no 3 (www.socresonline.org.uk/5/3/mulberg.html).

Office of Public Services Reform (2003) *Inspecting for improvement*, London: Cabinet Office.

O'Malley, P. (2000) 'Uncertain subjects: risks, liberalism and contract', *Economy and Society*, vol 29, no 4, pp 460-84.

O'Malley, P., Weir, L. and Shearing, C. (1997) 'Governmentality, criticism, politics', *Economy and Society*, vol 26, no 4, pp 501-17.

O'Neill, O. (2002) *A question of trust: The BBC Reith lectures 2002*, Cambridge: Cambridge University Press.

Osborne, D. and Gaebler, T. (1993) *Reinventing government: How the entrepreneurial spirit is transforming the public sector*, New York, NY: Penguin.

Parkin, F. (1972) *Class inequality and political order: Social stratification in capitalist and communist societies*, London: Paladin.

Parsons, T. (1949) 'Professions and social structure', in T. Parsons, *Essays in sociological theory*, New York, NY: The Free Press, pp 34-49.

Parsons, T. (1968) 'Professions', in *International encyclopedia of the social sciences, vol 12*, New York, NY: Macmillan and The Free Press, pp 536-47.

Pawson, R. and Tilley, N. (1997) *Realistic evaluation*, London: Sage Publications.

Peters, T. and Waterman, R. (1982) *In search of excellence: Lessons from America's best run companies*, New York, NY: Harper Collins.

Pollitt, C. (1988) 'Bringing consumers into performance measurement: concepts, consequences and constraints', *Policy & Politics*, vol 16, no 2, pp 77-87.

Pollitt, C. (1990) 'Doing business in the temple: managers and quality assurance in the public services', *Public Administration*, vol 68, no 4, pp 435-52.

Pollitt, C. (1993) *Managerialism and the public service: The Anglo-American experience*, Oxford: Blackwell Publishing.

Pollitt, C. and Bouckaert, G. (2004) *Public management reform: A comparative analysis*, Oxford: Oxford University Press.

Polyani, K. (1957) *The great transformation*, Boston, MA: Gower Beacon Press.

Power, M. (1997) *The audit society: Rituals of verification*, Oxford: Oxford University Press.

Productivity Commission (2003) *General practice administrative and compliance costs*, Melbourne: Productivity Commission.

Raeburn, N. (2004) *Changing corporate America from inside out: Lesbian and gay workplace rights*, Minneapolis, MN: University of Minnesota Press.

Ramsbotham, D. (2005) *Prisongate: The shocking state of British prisons and the need for visionary change*, London: Free Press.

Rankin, J. and Campbell, M. (2006) *Managing to nurse: Inside Canada's health care reform*, Toronto: University of Toronto Press.

Regulatory Impact Unit (2001) *Making a difference: Reducing general practitioner (GP) paperwork*, London: Cabinet Office.

Roberts, G. (2005) 'The evaluation of academic research in the United Kingdom', *Oxford Magazine, Eight Week, Trinity Term*, pp 7-10.

Robbins, A. (1997) *Unlimited power: The new science of personal achievement*, New York, NY: The Free Press.

Rock, P. (1994) 'The social organisation of a Home Office initiative', *European Journal of Crime, Criminal Law and Criminal Justice*, vol 2, no 2, pp 141-67.

Rock, P. (1995) 'The opening stages of criminal justice policymaking', *British Journal of Criminology*, vol 35, no 1, pp 1-16.

Rogers, C. (1983) *Freedom to learn for the 1980s*, Columbia, OH: C.E. Merrill.

Rose, N. (1996) 'The death of the social? Re-figuring the territory of government', *Economy and Society*, vol 25, no 3, pp 327-56.

Rose, N. and Miller, P. (1992) 'Political power beyond the state: problematics of government', *British Journal of Sociology*, vol 43, no 2, pp 173-205.

Salaman, G. (1995) *Managing*, Buckingham: Open University Press.

Salter, B. (2004) *The new politics of medicine*, Basingstoke: Palgrave.

Sampson, A. (2004) *Who runs this place? Anatomy of Britain in the 21st century*, London: John Murray.

Sayer, D. (1991) Capitalism and modernity: An excursus on Marx and Weber, London: Routledge.

Schick, A. (1969) 'Systems politics and systems budgeting', *Public Administrative Review*, vol 29, no 2, pp 137-51.

Schutz, A. (1973) *Collected papers I: The problem of social reality*, The Hague: Martinus Nijhoff.

Seddon, J. (2000) *The case against ISO 9000*, Dublin: Oak Tree Press.

Sennett, R. (2006) *The culture of the new capitalism*, New Haven, CT: Yale University Press.

Shore, C. and Wright, S. (2000) 'Coercive accountability: the rise of audit culture in higher education', in M. Strathern (ed) *Audit cultures: Anthropological studies in accountability, ethics and the academy*, London: Routledge, pp 57-89.

Sieber, S. (1981) *Fatal remedies*, New York, NY: Plenum Press.

Sinclair, J., Ironside, M. and Siefert, R. (1996) 'Classroom struggle? Market-oriented reforms and their impact on the teacher labour process', *Work, Employment and Society*, vol 10, no 4, pp 641-61.

Skelcher, C. (1992) *Managing for service quality*, Harlow: Longman.

Skolnick, J. (1967) *Justice without trial: Law enforcement in democratic society*, New York, NY: Wiley.

Smith, D. (2005) *Institutional ethnography: A sociology for people*, Lanham, MD: Rowman and Littlefield.

Sommerlad, H. (1999) 'The implementation of quality initiatives and the new public management in the legal aid sector in England and Wales: bureaucratisation, stratification and surveillance', *International Journal of the Legal Profession*, vol 6, no 1, pp 311-40.

Sommerlad, H. (2001) '"I've lost the plot": an everyday story of legal aid lawyers', *Journal of Law and Society*, vol 28, no 3, pp 335-60.

Spector, M. and Kistuse, J. (1977) *Constructing social problems*, New York, NY: Aldine de Gruyter.

Stenson, K. (1998) 'Beyond histories of the present', *Economy and Society*, vol 27, no 4, pp 333-52.

Strathern, M. (ed) (2000) *Audit cultures: Anthropological studies in accountability, ethics and the academy*, London: Routledge.

Strauss, A. (1993) *Continual permutations of action*, New York, NY: Aldine de Gruyter.

Strauss, A. and Corbin, J. (1998) *Basics of qualitative research: Grounded theory procedures and techniques*, London: Sage Publications.

Sudnow, D. (1965) 'Normal crimes: sociological features of the penal code in a public defender office', *Social Problems*, vol 12, no 3, pp 255-76.

Taylor, F. (1990) 'Scientific management', in D. Pugh (ed) *Organisation theory: Selected readings* (first published 1947), Harmondsworth: Penguin, pp 203-22.

Tenner, A. and DeToro, I. (1992) *Total quality management: Three steps to continuous improvement*, Reading, MA: Addison-Wesley.

Thomas, G. (1999) 'Standards and school inspection: the rhetoric and the reality', in C. Cullingford (ed) *An inspector calls: Ofsted and its effect on school standards*, London: Kogan Page, pp 135-47.

Thompson, P. (1983) *The nature of work: An introduction to debates on the labour process*, Basingstoke: Macmillan.

Timmermans, S. and Berg, M. (2003) *The gold standard: The challenge of evidence-based medicine and standardisation in health care*, Philadelphia, PA: Temple University Press.

Travers, M. (1994) 'Measurement and reality: quality assurance and the work of a firm of criminal defence solicitors in northern England', *International Journal of the Legal Profession*, vol 1, no 2, pp 173-89.

Travers, M. (1997) *The reality of law: Work and talk in a firm of criminal lawyers*, Aldershot: Ashgate.

Travers, M. (1999) *The British immigration courts: A study of law and politics*, Bristol: The Policy Press.

Travers, M. (2004) 'The philosophical assumptions of constructionism', in K. Jacobs, J. Kemeny and T. Manzi (eds) *Social constructionism in housing research*, Aldershot: Ashgate, pp 14-31.

Travers, M. (2005a) 'Evaluation research and criminal justice: beyond a political critique', *Australian and New Zealand Journal of Criminology*, vol 38, no 1, pp 39-58.

Travers, M. (2005b) 'Evaluation research and legal services', in R. Banakar and M. Travers (eds) *Theory and method in socio-legal research*, Oxford: Hart, pp 327-48.

Tsutsui, W. (1998) *Manufacturing ideology: Scientific management in twentieth century Japan*, Princeton, NJ: Princeton University Press.

US Department of Labor (2002) 'Briefing: Office of Information and Regulatory Affairs', Washington (www.dol.gov/cio, accessed 23 January 2006).

Voehl, F. (ed) (1995) *Deming: The way we knew him*, Delray Beach, FL: St. Lucie Press.

Walsh, K. (1991) 'Quality and the public services', *Public Administration*, vol 69, no 4, pp 503-14.

Walsh, K. (1995) 'Quality through markets: the new public management', in A. Wilkinson and H. Willmott (eds) *Making quality critical: New perspectives on organisational change*, London: Routledge.

Weber, M. (1991) 'Bureaucracy', in H. Gerth and C. Wright Mills (eds) *From Max Weber*, London: Routledge, pp 196-244.

Weiss, C. (1998) *Evaluation: Methods for studying programs and policies* (2nd edn), Upper Saddle River, NJ: Prentice-Hall.

Wheeler, S. (1976) *On record: Files and dossiers in American life*, New Brunswick, NJ: Transaction Books.

Whyte, W. (1956) *The organisation man*, Garden City, NY: Doubleday.

Wiener, C. (2000) *The elusive quest: Accountability in hospitals*, New York, NY: Aldine de Gruyter.

Wilding, P. (1992) 'The British welfare state: Thatcherism's enduring legacy', *Policy & Politics*, vol 20, no 2, pp 201-11.

Wiles, P. (2002) 'Criminology in the 21st century: public good or private interest? The Sir John Barry memorial lecture', *Australian and New Zealand Journal of Criminology*, vol 35, no 2, pp 238-52.

Wilkinson, A. and Willmott, H. (1995) *Making quality critical: New perspectives on organizational change*, London: Routledge.

Witz, A. (1992) *Professions and patriarchy*, London: Routledge.

Woodhead, C. (1998) *Blood on the tracks: Lessons from the history of education reform*, London: Ofsted.

Wragg, T. (2003) 'Soapbox', *Times Higher Education Supplement*, 19 December, p 8.

Zifcak, S. (1994) *New managerialism: Administrative reform in Whitehall and Canberra*, Buckingham: Open University Press.

Index

Note: Page numbers in *italic* refer to figures.